Blair's Educational Legacy?

The United Kingdom General Election on 1st May 1997 gave a landslide victory to a re-vitalised Labour Party. Tony Blair became Prime Minister with a huge Commons majority of 179 over all other parties. Such a majority meant that extensive changes of policy could be implemented with little effective opposition.

During the election campaign Tony Blair had repeatedly claimed that the top three priorities of a New Labour government would be 'education, education, education', and on page two of the Labour Party's election manifesto a smiling Blair is seen with Nelson Mandela - the unacknowledged originator of the oratorical education triplet. Following a third Election victory in 2005 and after over ten years as Prime Minister, Blair finally stepped down to Gordon Brown in mid-2007, but only after a promotional 'final tour' that lasted several months. Towards the end, Blair devoted considerable efforts to try to ensure that his legacy would be positive and that he would be remembered for more than his role in the Iraq war.

But what is his legacy in the field of education? This book brings together the assessments of key educational researchers who have been centrally involved with both the critique and implementation of various policy developments. It is now time to make a solid academic evaluation of his influence on education. This book is timely, and relates directly to the central policy themes of the last decade. It considers the relationships between theory and practice and examines the nature of policy and politics. Each contribution will review empirical data and policy changes relating to Blair's period as Prime Minister and will make an assessment of the enduring effects of changes in policy. Each will assess the long-term and lasting effects as well as the shorter-term responses.

This book was published as a special issue of the *Oxford Review of Education*.

Geoffrey Walford is Professor of Education Policy and Fellow of Green Templeton College at the University of Oxford.

Blair's Educational Legacy?

Edited by Geoffrey Walford

Routledge
Taylor & Francis Group
LONDON AND NEW YORK

First published 2010 by Routledge

Published 2016 by Routledge
2 Park Square, Milton Park, Abingdon, Oxfordshire OX14 4RN
711 Third Avenue, New York, NY 10017

First issued in paperback 2016

Routledge is an imprint of the Taylor & Francis Group, an informa business

Typeset in Plantin by Value Chain, India

British Library Cataloguing in Publication Data
A catalogue record for this book is available from the British Library

ISBN 13: 978-1-138-96479-2 (pbk)
ISBN 13: 978-0-415-48305-6 (hbk)

CONTENTS

Abstracts

Tony Blair, the promotion of the 'active' educational citizen, and middle-class hegemony

DIANE REAY

Tony Blair's period as Head of the Labour Government from 1997 until 2007 has been heralded as a period of increased parental power and growing choice within education. However, beneath the rhetoric, Blair's legacy has been one of consolidating and re-inforcing previous Conservative policies that stressed parental responsibilities whilst operating with a white middle-class norm. As a result, inequalities between parents have grown under Blair as working-class parents are positioned as failing, and middle-class parents monopolise educational initiatives initially set up to benefit the disadvantaged.

Zero tolerance of failure and New Labour approaches to school improvement in England

PAM SAMMONS

Under the leadership of Tony Blair New Labour committed itself to raise standards, tackle educational failure and use education to combat disadvantage. This paper examines New Labour's approaches to school improvement, particularly the origins and enactment of 'zero tolerance' strategies, the different groups of schools identified as needing remedial action, different intervention strategies for poorly performing and failing schools including inspection, Fresh Start, Academies and the London Challenge. It explores evidence of their impact on school improvement, educational standards and equity.

Academies and diplomas: two strategies for shaping the future workforce

RICHARD HATCHER

The unprecedented extent of privatisation of provision in the school system on a for-profit basis is clearly one of the most significant transformations accomplished by the Blair government. However, another aspect of private sector involvement has proved much more problematic: the direct involvement of employers in the formation of the future workforce, in two forms: employerled vocationally-oriented diplomas and state schools—Academies—run by business interests. Both strategies remain key policies of the Brown government and have been endorsed by the Conservative opposition. However, whether these two strategies can provide the basis of a stable policy settlement depends upon the extent to which they prove capable of delivering the 'human capital' the economy is claimed to require. This paper assesses the evidence.

14–19

RICHARD PRING

Developing a coherent 14–19 phase of education and training has been a major feature of the last ten years of the Labour government. This has been the case, too, of the Welsh Assembly Government since its establishment in 1999 with its separate education policy and arrangement. The English 'project' might be characterised by (i) a more holistic approach to the total welfare of the young person, reflected in the attempt to join up the various services which affect welfare in general and educational achievement in particular; (ii) the 'personalisation' of learning; (iii) collaboration or partnership between the different providers of education and training; (iv) a reform of the whole system of qualifications; (v) a revamp of the training and apprenticeship system; and (vi) increased central 'management' of the system to ensure targets are reached. The Welsh 'project' has been different in many respects—an interesting contrast as the two systems increasingly diverge.

Faith-based schools in England after ten years of Tony Blair

GEOFFREY WALFORD

While faith schools have always been an integral part of the English state-maintained system of education, during Tony Blair's period as Prime Minister there was a distinct encouragement of the sector. This article assesses the long-term effects of such support.

Realising the potential of new technology? Assessing the legacy of New Labour's ICT agenda 1997–2007

NEIL SELWYN

'Realising the potential of new technology' was one of the central educational themes of New Labour's 1997 election manifesto, with 'information and communications technology' (ICT) established subsequently as a prominent feature of the Blair administration policy portfolio. As such New Labour can claim rightly to have made an unprecedented and sustained political commitment to technology in education, directing over £5 billion of funding towards educational ICT during the 1997 to 2007 period. Yet the fact remains that the New Labour ICT agenda has failed to achieve the much promised technological 'transformation' of the UK education system. With this in mind the present paper develops the argument that New Labour's concern with educational ICT was driven primarily by concerns over enhancing competitiveness in a globalising economy, creating a lifelong learning system fit for a successful knowledge economy and modernising the formal education sector. Thus whilst New Labour's ICT agenda may well have had the short term impact of increasing the physical presence of ICT resources in all education institutions, its longer-term educational legacy was compromised by the wider macro-level issues it purported to address. As such the legacy of this high-profile segment of policy-making should be seen primarily in terms of establishing ICT as an ideological presence in the UK education system.

Tony Blair and the politics of race in education: whiteness, doublethink and New Labour

DAVID GILLBORN

It is tempting to view the Blairite legacy as a simple story of political hypocrisy: a government, swept to power after almost two decades of Conservative rule, promising much but reneging on those commitments and falling back on Thatcherite authoritarian popularism when the going got tough. But that would be too simple a story. The Blairite policy trajectory in relation to race and education reveals problems that are much more deep-rooted, and more significant, than mere political opportunism. The failure to address racism as a structural factor that shapes the assumptions of the education system (embodied in notions of selection, ability and discipline) made possible, maybe even inevitable, a situation where race equality would be sacrificed to the perceived interests and sensitivities of White people.

Making teaching a 21st century profession: Tony Blair's big prize

JOHN FURLONG

From his very earliest days in office, Tony Blair believed that if he was to achieve his broader educational reforms then the teaching profession itself needed modernising—it had to become a '21st century profession'. This paper charts the background to this aspiration and the complex range of interrelated policies used to achieve that reform. They included: a changed role for initial teacher education; a more differentiated workforce; strategies to 'focus' professionalism (appraisal, standards and CPD); and a redefinition of professional knowledge. Through these policies, the Government hoped to harness teacher professionalism to their broader reform agenda. The paper concludes with a discussion of Tony Blair's legacy in this field both in England and internationally.

Beyond tuition fees? The legacy of Blair's government to higher education

INGRID LUNT

Although the famous Blair mantra 'education, education, education' was applied by his government mainly to the compulsory education sector, there was no shortage of initiatives in Higher Education (HE). The scene was set by the Dearing Report in 1997 which effectively determined the direction of Blair's first term. The second term enabled Blair to pursue further an agenda of public sector reform, yet the simultaneous commitment to market principles of choice and diversity and to social inclusion created major tensions and dilemmas. Funding the expanded HE was the stimulus which led to Dearing, and has continued to be the major challenge of the ten-year period.

New Labour, education and Wales: the devolution decade

DAVID REYNOLDS

An account is given of the development of a distinctive set of education policies in Wales after devolution of power in 1999. In contrast to policies in England that emphasised consumer choice concerning accountability, and central state 'support' of the profession, Wales chose a more 'producerist' paradigm that emphasised collaboration between educational partners. Differences between the two societies are also in evidence concerning levels of expenditure, and the role of local authorities as delivery mechanisms. Performance data do not suggest that Wales has improved more rapidly than England, although there are considerable difficulties in making these kinds of assessments. Conclusions are drawn concerning the legacy of Welsh educational change for the New Labour/Blairite paradigm.

Evaluating 'Blair's Educational Legacy?': some comments on the special issue of Oxford Review of Education

GEOFF WHITTY

The December 2008 special issue of the *Oxford Review of Education* provided a review of education policy during Tony Blair's tenure as Prime Minister. This paper forms a response to the ten contributions to that special issue and discusses some of the issues raised in them. While a few positive aspects of education under New Labour were identified in the special edition, it focused more on the failures of New Labour than its achievements. A common theme to emerge from the papers included the government's pursuit of neo-liberal market policies at the expense of its professed commitment to social justice. While accepting that the government's failure to tackle the differences in educational outcomes between advantaged and disadvantaged pupils constitutes a major failing, the present author argues that significant achievements, such as early years provision, were neglected in the special issue. He also discusses the electoral considerations facing New Labour and the personal role of Tony Blair in determining policy. The paper goes on to consider whether New Labour's education policy has changed since the departure of Blair and identifies some hints of a potentially more progressive approach developing under Brown. It concludes by suggesting that contributing towards a debate about alternatives to Blairite policies should now become a priority for the 'educational establishment'.

Notes on Contributors

John Furlong is Director of the Department of Education in the University of Oxford. A former President of BERA and member of the 2008 RAE Panel, John Furlong has led a wide range of research projects on teacher education and teacher professionalism. In 2006 he chaired the Review of Initial Teacher Education Provision in Wales (the Furlong Report) on behalf of the Welsh Assembly Government.

David Gillborn is Professor of Education at the Institute of Education, London, and editor of the international journal *Race Ethnicity and Education.* His recent publications include *Racism & Education: coincidence or conspiracy?* (Routledge, 2008).

Richard Hatcher is Director of research in the Faculty of Education at Birmingham City University. He has written widely on education policy issues. He is a coauthor of *Schooling in Western Europe: the new order and its adversaries*, published in 2008.

Ingrid Lunt is Professor of Educational Studies at the Department of Education, University of Oxford. From 1999–2005 she was Head (Dean) of the Doctoral School at the Institute of Education, University of London. She served on the ESRC Training and Development Board 2001–2005. She has a particular interest in doctoral education, and the relationship between professional knowledge and the university, and is the co-author of Scott, D., Brown, A., Lunt, I. & Thorne, L. (2004) *Professional doctorates: integrating professional and academic knowledge* (Open University Press and SRHE).

Richard Pring is presently Lead Director of Nuffield Review 14–19 Education and Training England and Wales, the report of which will be published in May 2009.

David Reynolds is Professor of Education at the University of Plymouth, and has published widely on school effectiveness, school improvement and teacher effectiveness. He has also been heavily involved in national educational policymaking through chairing the Numeracy Task Force, being a Board Member of BECTA and the TTA/TDA, and being a 0.2 Adviser to the Department of Children, Families and Schools from 1999 to 2006. He lives in Wales.

Diane Reay is a Professor of Education in the Faculty of Education, University of Cambridge, with particular interests in social justice issues in education, Pierre Bourdieu's social theory, and cultural analyses of social class. She has researched extensively in the areas of social class, gender and ethnicity across primary, secondary and post-compulsory stages of education.

Neil Selwyn is based at the London Knowledge Lab as part of the Institute of Education, University of London. His research and teaching focuses on the sociology of education technology, with recent work addressing the areas of digital exclusion, education technology policymaking and the student experience of technology-based learning.

Pam Sammons is a Professor of Education at the Department of Education, University of Oxford. Her research studies include investigations of school and teacher effectiveness and school improvement. She is also interested in policy evaluation, promoting equity and the study of educational disadvantage. She is author/coauthor of *School effectiveness and equity: making connections*; *Teachers matter: connecting lives, work and effectiveness*; *Improvement through inspection*; *evaluating the impact of Ofsted*; *School effectiveness: coming of age in the 21st century*; *Forging links: effective schools and effective departments*; and *School matters: the junior years*.

Geoffrey Walford is a Fellow of Green Templeton College and Professor of Education Policy at the University of Oxford. He is Editor of the *Oxford Review of Education*.

Geoff Whitty has been Director of the Institute of Education, University of London, since September 2000. His main areas of teaching and research are the sociology of education, education policy and teacher education. His publications include *Making Sense of Education Policy* (Sage, 2002) and *Education and the Middle Class* (with Sally Power, Tony Edwards and Valerie Wigfall) (Open University Press, 2003). He is a past President of the British Educational Research Association and currently a specialist advisor to the House of Commons Children, Schools and Families Committee.

Introduction

Geoffrey Walford

1st May 1997 was a beautiful sunny day. I well remember walking across University Parks to my office in the morning sunshine and everyone I met seemed to be smiling. At long last the Conservative Government had been replaced and Tony Blair was Britain's new Prime Minister. As an educationalist, I was particularly excited by Blair's now well-known three top policy priorities—education, education and education.

Just over ten years later, Blair left office. Had his promise to prioritise education come to anything? What is his educational legacy? This collection of contributions seeks to give some preliminary answers to these questions. Each of the ten articles takes a particular area of education policy and gives an evaluation of what has been accomplished and what might be the longer-term legacy. The final chapter of this book is a response, by Geoff Whitty, to the ten previous chapters which also considers the extent of policy change since Blair left office.

Such a collection cannot be comprehensive. There are many other possible topics that could have been covered and, indeed, some others were included in an earlier Special Issue of the *Oxford Review of Education* which reviewed Blair's first two terms of office (Walford, 2005). Space constraints also mean that all of the contributions are necessarily short. However, the collection does present an important assessment of what was achieved and how Blair's terms of office might be viewed in the future.

References

Walford, G. (2005) (Ed.) Education and the Labour Government: an evaluation of two terms. Special Issue, *Oxford Review of Education,* 31(1).

Tony Blair, the promotion of the 'active' educational citizen, and middle-class hegemony

Diane Reay

Introduction

Tony Blair's last months in office became a period in which his legacy was conspicuously celebrated—in a variety of high profile speeches, visits, and finally a world tour. The real legacy, not just of Tony Blair the politician but of New Labour more generally, is both more complex and more problematic. New Labour, under Tony Blair's leadership, entered into a Faustian pact with the forces of neoliberalism (Beck, 2008) and it is the twists and turns of this alignment, and its consequences for social justice, that the paper explores in relation to parents and education. As John Beck (2008) points out, the irony of New Labour policy under Blair's tutelege is that despite the constant rhetoric around choice and, in particular, parental choice, it led more generally to the eradication of the range of effective political choice in 21st-century Britain and especially England. More specifically, in relation to parents and education, it could be argued that it has led to the reinvention of the past in the present. It is misleading on a number of levels to talk in terms of Blair's own personal legacy when it comes to parents and education. Rather, it has been argued that he entrenched

Thatcherism (Baker, 2007). And in many ways Blair has trod a well worn path, following in the steps of Old Tory policies as much as he has forged a 'new' Third Way in educational policy. In the next section I outline a brief history of parental involvement in education over the past 50 years before turning to the rhetoric and realities of educational policy in relation to parents under Blair's leadership.

A brief history of parental involvement in schooling

There have been enormous changes over the past 50 years in the relationship between home and school. Where once there was a clearly defined separation between the two in which schools made very few educational demands of parents, now we have a situation in which it is the expectation that all parents will become involved in their children's schooling. The importance of close links between teachers and parents in promoting children's achievement was first recognised in the 1960s. The establishment of Education Priority Areas, set up in the late 1960s, saw the appointment of home–school liaison teachers with explicit responsibility for promoting home–school links (Halsey, 1972).

More recently, under a Conservative administration led by Margaret Thatcher, partnership between parents and teachers became enshrined in educational policy (DES, 1985, 1988). The 1985 White Paper *Better Schools* emphasised the importance of home–school links, and urged that schools should explain their aims and policies to parents and associate parents with their work. Three years later the 1988 Education Reform Act promised parents much more information, through league tables, about the performance of schools and individual pupils. A recurring theme throughout the Act was that of accountability to parents. Parents were to be encouraged to become consumers within education. A further aspect of this consumer orientation lay in the promotion of parental choice. Parents were to be allowed to choose the best school to suit their children's educational needs. The reality, however, has been somewhat different to the policy rhetoric. Since the inception of the policy there has been a growing body of research which demonstrates that educational markets are class and race-biased. 'Parents seem to make choices on the basis of the perceived class and, in some instances, racial composition of schools' (Gewirtz *et al.*, 1995, p. 184).

The growing consumer-orientated perspective was particularly evident in the 1991 Parent's Charter. Under the Charter parental rights to information about schools and their own children's progress and results in the context of wider performance would be mandatory. In addition, the Charter made clear to parents that they too had responsibilities. By 1991, the whole approach to parent–school relations had shifted from one about how to ensure some measures of equity to how to ensure parental rights and responsibilities (David, 1993). Perhaps the best summation of the state-of-play in relation to parental involvement at the beginning of the 1990s was provided by Philip Brown:

> We are entering a 'third wave' ... which is neither part of a final drive to 'meritocracy', nor the result of a socialist victory for educational reform. To date, the 'third wave' has been

> characterised by the rise of the educational parentocracy, where a child's education is increasingly dependent on the wealth and wishes of parents, rather than the ability and efforts of pupils ... the ideology of parentocracy involves a major programme of educational privatisation under the slogans of 'parental choice', 'educational standards', and the 'free market'. (1990, pp. 66–67)

So prior to Blair's election in 1997 there was a growing emphasis on the accountability of both teachers and parents. During the 1990s parental involvement was officially recognised as a key factor in school improvement and effectiveness (Reynolds & Cuttance, 1992), and in 1994 became a requisite part of a school's development plan (Ofsted, 1994). Ofsted guidelines issued the following year (1995, p. 98) outlined a model of parents and teachers working together to provide support at home. So Blair inherited a political culture where choice was seen as central to educational policy, and parents were increasingly constituted as key to improving schools.

New Labour or Old Tory?

In 1997 when Tony Blair was elected Prime Minister the precepts driving New Labour educational policy were three-fold: first, efforts to identify what makes some schools more effective than others, followed by the development of school improvement initiatives aimed at making every school an effective school. Second came the imposition of the standards agenda—involving the use of ever-rising attainment targets and the development within schools of a culture of 'performativity' (Ball, 2003a). A third key element has involved decisively breaking with the so-called 'one size fits all' policy of comprehensive schooling, in favour of a far more differentiated system of secondary schooling (Tomlinson, 2005). All three aspects of New Labour policy were underpinned by the need for parents to behave as 'rational' and responsible consumers of education. The New Labour aspiration was that parents could, to a much greater extent than was possible in the past, exercise significant choice in the type of school they preferred for their children. However, there remained key continuities and these were recognised by Blair in the Labour Party Manifesto of 1997 (p. 3) which asserted, 'Some things the Conservative party got right. We will not change them'.

The antecedents of old Tory policy were clearly visible in the intensification of the move from parental rights to increased parental responsibilities initiated under the previous Conservative administration. Collaboration between home and school seems to have been superseded by the colonisation of the home by the school (Edwards & Warin, 1999). This attempt to turn homes into extensions of school learning environments was exemplified in statutory home–school agreements introduced in 1999, despite considerable disquiet from both educationalists and parent groups. According to the Government White Paper *Excellence in Cities* (DfEE, 1998):

> all schools should, in discussion with parents develop a home-school contract. These agreements will reflect the respective responsibilities of home and school in raising standards, stating clearly what is expected of the school, of the parent and the pupil.

With the home–school agreement policy, the expectation that all parents would engage in 'home–school work' with their children became normative and part of commonsense understanding about what being a parent involved (Crozier, 2000). Parents were expected to carry out a range of tasks, for example supervising homework, attending school meetings and providing the correct equipment, as well as offering unconditional support to the school (Crozier & Reay, 2005). As Stephen Ball (2003b) argues, the range of recent educational policies which emphasise parenting roles and empower parents in relation to schools have made the boundary between the private domestic sphere and the public sphere of schooling increasingly porous. One consequence is that we now have a paradoxical situation in which the public sphere, including education, is increasingly being privatised, while the private sphere of the home is increasingly being publicly regulated and activities within it held up for scrutiny and judgement. Under Blair, school and schooling made even greater inroads into the home and family life in what McNamara *et al.* (2000, p. 474) have labelled 'the Blairite project of Total Schooling'.

Parents under Blair were regularly tasked with becoming their children's educators alongside teachers. So in 1999 David Blunkett, the then Secretary of State for Education, told the CBI 'we need parents who are prepared to take responsibility for supporting their children's education'. This colonisation of home by schooling was also made explicit in the Labour Party Manifesto for 2005 which asserted:

> Our plan now is to tailor our education system to individual pupil needs, with parents supporting teachers and support staff in further raising standards. (p. 32)

Here parents are clearly positioned as teaching adjuncts, as educational labourers increasingly responsible for their own children's academic progress but also collectively for improving schools and raising standards. This simultaneous redrawing and blurring of the boundaries between household economies and the new developing market economy in state schooling potentially increases the workload and the spending of all families. What is uncontestable is that supporting schooling has had a substantial economic impact on families. In 2003 for the first time in the history of state schooling parents were spending more per annum on textbooks than their children's schools were (Townsend, 2003). There has also been an exponential growth in private tuition and commercial books for home learning (Buckingham & Scanlon, 2003).

According to John Hutton, former Work and Pensions Secretary, Tony Blair's greatest achievement was in ensuring that the marketisation of the public services is now built into the DNA of public service provision (Chitty, 2007). But in relation to education the relentless marketisation of the field has resulted in it being increasingly perceived as an arena of intense competition by growing numbers of parents. So Scanlon and Buckingham (2004, p. 301) found that 'the majority of parents they interviewed about out-of-school learning experienced increasing stress and pressure over their children's education'. Parental anxiety over schooling has grown in intensity as parents, with varying degrees of enthusiasm, engage with school choice and take up the role of home educators. This parental anxiety, generated by the new consumerist, highly competitive, choice-led educational market, crosses class and ethnic differences. But as I examine in more detail in the section below, the ability to take up these new parental positions—as active chooser and parent educator—is differentially distributed according to social class.

Blair's Parentocracy: the creation of 'new' educational inequalities

As well as increasing levels of stress and anxiety for all parents, being positioned as 'home educators' also compounds existing educational inequalities between families. The current political preoccupation with parental involvement in education is underpinned by an assumption that all parents share an identical experience of involvement in their children's schooling. We have a discourse of parenting in which gendered, racialised and classed notions of parent are not acknowledged, rendering inequalities existing between parents invisible.

It is vital, therefore, to stress that both parental involvement in schooling and parental choice are classed, 'raced' and gendered processes. If we take gender first, government education policy works with an homogeneous notion of 'parent' which fails to recognise the gendered division of labour operating in the home with respect to parental involvement. This failure to recognise gender continues despite recent empirical research demonstrating that it is predominantly mothers who are 'the most involved parent' (Crozier, 2000; Vincent & Ball, 2006). Fathers are far more likely to be 'helping hands' rather than equal partners in their child's education. Minority ethnic differences are also neglected, despite research (Bhatti, 2000; Crozier, 2005) that shows that minority ethnic parents often feel their relationship to the educational system is one of protector, underpinned by 'the need to defend, rescue and protect their child' (Crozier, 2005, p. 55) from an education system they perceive to be racist.

The actual processes of parental involvement and choice then are very different to the Blairite rhetoric. They are characterised by continuing inequalities of gender, race and social class (Blanden & Machin, 2007). In particular, the enormous growth in private tuition (Russell, 2002; Scanlon & Buckingham, 2004) and educational activities out of school (Vincent & Ball, 2006) are enabled by middle-class processes of 'out-sourcing' on the part of a class grouping that is time-poor and resource-rich. In contrast, few working-class parents can afford the cost of hiring private tutors and sending children to Kumon maths classes even if they have the inclination.

In addition to increasing the flow of educational work into the home, the Blair administration has also expanded the arena of parental choice. Choice became a repeated mantra throughout the Blair years, for example in the 2005 schools White Paper *Higher Standards, Better Schools for All*, where power for parents is a key theme. Here too Blair throughout his tenure seemed unable to recognise and understand that parents bring very different levels of inclination and resources to their choice of, and involvement in, schooling. As a consequence, New Labour policies, no less than old Tory ones, were based on a notion of the 'ideal' parent, that all parents could and should aspire to, when in reality this ideal parent was in effect one with middle-class resources, dispositions and values. There is an extensive research both here and in the

USA that indicates that middle-class parents are strongly inclined to choice (Reay, 1998; Gewirtz, 2001; Ball, 2003b; Brantlinger, 2003; André-Bechely, 2005). However, in earlier research with Stephen Ball and Helen Lucey we found this was not the case for many working-class parents whose preference was for a good local school, and who had little inclination to play the educational market (Reay & Ball, 1997; Reay & Lucey, 2003). Yet, New Labour under Blair has legislated to increase parental choice, moves premised on the notion that all parents both want, and have the necessary resources to choose the 'best' schools for their children. This universalising of what Sharon Gewirtz (2001, p. 368) calls 'the ideal-typical middle-class parents of the New Labour imagination' has resulted in a reassertion of the power of the middle class to corner what is best for its children, much of it disguised as the exercise of parental choice. And a growing body of research (Burgess *et al.*, 2005; Reay *et al.*, 2005) has demonstrated that choice systems promote rather than ameliorate educational inequalities. As I have argued in earlier work (Reay, 2006), it is here we see powerful continuities with the past as the Blair government maintained the means for middle-class families to gain educational advantages and separate themselves off from class and racialised others. Parental choice, in particular, has above all been a response to middle-class concerns (Ball, 2008).

Education for the sake of the economy

As Blair asserted in a speech delivered in 2005, 'education is our best economic policy', and the role of education under Blair has increasingly become one of responding to, and redressing the impact of international economic competition (Mulderrig, 2003). The idea was that greater choice would spur increased competition between schools which would then lead to improvements in efficiency within the educational sector itself, but also more widely within the economy. However, as Gibbons *et al.* (2006) argue, there is little evidence of any link between choice and achievement, while there is evidence that increased competition has resulted in greater stratification. Where Blair has succeeded is in further entrenching Thatcherite discourses which see education neither as an entitlement nor an end in its own right, but as a means to enhancing economic growth and proficiency, transforming parents' work in support of their children's schooling into an economic as well as an educational activity.

Blair sees a similar role for education within the social sphere, arguing that 'education has a unique ability to correct the inequalities of class or background' (Blair, 2006). This is the exact opposite of Basil Bernstein's succinct assessment of 1970 that 'education cannot compensate for society'. Rather, under Blair education was to compensate for, and make good, the ills of both society and the economy. In this instrumentalising of education parents are positioned as drivers not only of educational improvement but also of economic and social resurgence and vitality.

As part of this project, they are expected to embody responsible active citizenship. Just as Baker (1998) found in relation to 'the child', the parent, within Blairite policy making, has become a political space for the production of neo-liberal rationalities and technologies concerned with active and responsible citizenship. Parents are to be persuaded to act on their own behalf and, as Baez and Talburt (2008, p. 27) argue, they are to be 'the chief means of achieving the objectives of two neo-liberal projects; creating responsible, self-reliant citizens and making schools more efficient'. Often in Blair's speeches and texts (Blair, 1998, 2005, 2006) there is a logic of empowerment that masks a 'responsibilisation' of the parent. So in his 2005 speech on education reform he claimed 'in our schools, the system will finally be opened up to real parent power'. This seeming empowerment of parents as partners in their children's learning is, in effect, a delegation of work previously undertaken in the school.

Winners and losers in the educational field

Pupils of different abilities are now less likely to be educated together even in schools that are supposed to be socially mixed. In the ESRC Social Identities project on the white middle classes and urban comprehensives (Reay *et al.*, 2007) we found that the white middle classes dominated top sets and gifted and talented programmes in socially mixed comprehensives. As one mother explained, her initial concerns about poor behaviour and ill-discipline had been ill-founded because her daughter's comprehensive 'is very much like two schools in that, you know, if you're in the top sets you're in one school, it's a bit like grammar and secondary modern all in one school'. Under New Labour the middle classes have also used their market advantage to take up places in new educational initiatives. As a result the working classes are disproportionately under-represented in the very academic programmes, such as Excellence in Cities and Gifted and Talented, aimed at developing their educational success (Machin *et al.*, 2006; Araujo, 2007). Almost all the white middle-class children in our sample had been included in Gifted and Talented programmes where the school had one. In the quote below another mother talks about her feelings of amusement when her son was chosen, along with other top-set pupils at his poorly performing comprehensive, to have a university mentor to encourage him to think about going to university:

> Now, I'm not quite sure why they chose him. There's a few of them that have been chosen, but they obviously think that he's suitable. The thing is, my expectation is that he's going to go to university anyway [laughs]. (Gill Harris, mother, Riverton)

Choice policy under New Labour has further empowered middle-class parents (Ball, 2003b; Vincent & Ball, 2006), but it has had quite the reverse impact on working-class parents. As Ball (2008) points out, while programmes like Sure Start are educational in the sense of giving children a good start in learning, they are also disciplinary in so far as they are also about early interventions into what are perceived to be dysfunctional families. Recent evidence (Belsky *et al.*, 2006; Astle, 2007) has shown that Sure Start overwhelmed and alienated working-class mothers leaving middle-class families to reap the benefits of extra provision and funding.

The thrust of Blair's educational policy has been to enable middle-class parents to 'govern' themselves, although accompanied by increasing levels of anxiety (Rose,

1999). Working-class parents are much more likely to be subject to 'governance' in education as the conduct of working-class parents and their children has been problematised and then become the object of regulative intervention. Regulations, introduced in 2002 and strengthened in 2006, established parenting contracts and orders that made parents responsible for pupil truancy and subject to prosecution leading to heavy fines or imprisonment. This is just one example of how working-class parents have been positioned under New Labour—as failing parents. They are portrayed as in need of re-education, intervention and ultimately coercion with respect to the 'good' discipline and 'proper' conduct of their children (Gillies, 2005).

For Blair the active, responsible, educational citizen is able to ensure their own children's educational success and good discipline. But the negative aspects to this Blairite promotion of active citizenship can be found in the results of the 2006 poll that found that 44% of parents would use underhand tactics to secure a place at a school they perceive to be 'good'. Middle-class practices which under Blair have epitomised 'good' parental behaviour have become part of the problem under the new choice regimes. More widely any responsibility the education system and Government may have for what many researchers have identified for the past 50 years as systemic problems (McCulloch, 1998) has been discharged onto 'failing' parents and 'failing' teachers. And while the middle-classes are the winners and successes of New Labour educational policy, working-class parents are its failures and their position as losers in the education game is construed as simply their own fault, a failure to make the 'right' choices. The dominance of choice discourses and neo-liberal notions of agency seem to have eradicated any understanding of wider structural forces (Hursh, 2004). Everyone is seen to be free to choose (Rose, 1999). It no longer appears possible to view working-class parents as unable to support their children educationally because of a lack of resources and/or their own negative experiences of schooling. Rather, they are seen to choose not to support their children or in relation to choice of school to make the 'wrong' choices. The failure to recognise that parental involvement in schooling and parental choice are classed, 'raced' and gendered processes has resulted in the growth rather than the alleviation of class inequalities one would expect under a Labour government. While Blair has understood the middle-class psyche very well because in many ways he epitomises it, he appears to be far less informed about working-class cultures and experiences.

Conclusion

> Taken together our findings suggest that simply offering parents a wider choice of schools and forcing schools to compete does not seem to be a remedy for poor standards in education; such a policy might also exacerbate inequalities. (Gibbons *et al.*, 2006)

Blair has perpetuated and reinforced the myths of Conservative thinking, whilst energising and expanding the scope of neo-liberal influence within education. In this sense Blair and his educational policies can be seen as a bridge between the past and the future, in which he has acted as a conduit for very old inequalities of social class to be reinvented in new, thriving forms; a very 'New Labour' perpetuation of educational inequalities. The importation of the work of the school into the home has exacerbated educational inequalities, while the thriving choice agenda has become an educational means for middle-class parents to increasingly monopolise what they perceive to be 'the best' for their children. However, as one of the parents in the ESRC project on the white middle classes choosing urban comprehensives asserted, 'all parents cannot chose the best because the best is an exclusive thing' (Reay, 2008).

Blair's legacy lies not only in his entrenching of neo-liberal educational philosophy and policies but is embodied in the men who have emerged as his inheritors. In view of the neo-liberal convergence within the political sphere it is unsurprising that his inheritance lies in both the Labour and Conservative parties. So Gordon Brown is presented as a different kind of New Labour leader but remains very much in Blair's neo-liberal image:

> ... the empowerment of each individual, and the idea of responsibility comes alive in new forms of active civic engagement. Out go old assumptions of individuals passively receiving services; think instead of the responsible parent, the informed patient, the active citizen ... who—with an extension of choice and voice, individual and collective—are taking control and driving change forward. (Brown, 2006)

In January 2008, David Cameron, the leader of the UK Conservative party, could have been defending Blair's own parental school choices along with his policies when he defended parents who suddenly find religion as their child reaches school age. 'I don't blame anyone who tries to get their children into a good school,' he said. 'Most people are doing so because it has an ethos and culture. I believe in active citizens' (Dowling, 2008). Both Brown and Cameron continue to espouse educational policies framed and driven by the brand of neo-liberal individualism that became Blair's hallmark. What is clear is that Blair and his inheritors across the political spectrum offer no radical solutions to educational inequality, in fact no solutions at all. And in Blair's case we have a trail of failed policies that, rather than reducing inequality, have sedimented and augmented middle-class advantage in the educational field, a sad record for any political leader but a travesty for a Labour one.

References

André-Bechely, L. (2005) Public school choice at the intersection of voluntary integration and not-so-good neighborhood schools: lessons from parents' experiences, *Educational Administration Quarterly*, 41(2), 267–305.

Araujo, M. (2007) 'Modernising the comprehensive principle': selection, setting and the institutionalisation of educational failure, *British Journal of Sociology of Education,* 28(2), 241–257.
Astle, J. (2007) *The surest route: early years education and life chances* (London, CentreForum).
Baez, B. & Talburt, S. (2008) Governing for responsibility and with love: parents and children between home and school, *Educational Theory,* 58(1), 25–34.
Baker, B. (1998) 'Childhood' in the emergence and spread of US public schools, in: T. Popkewitz & M. Brennan (Eds) *Foucault's challenge: discourse, knowledge, and power in education* (New York, Teachers College Press).
Baker, M. (2007) Blair's legacy for schools. Available online at: http://news.bbc.co.uk/2/hi/uk_news/education/4996946.stm (accessed 6 February 2008).
Ball, S.J. (2003a) The teachers' soul and the terrors of performativity, *Journal of Education Policy,* 18(2), 215–228.
Ball, S.J. (2003b) *Class strategies and the educational market: the middle-classes and social advantage* (London, Routledge).
Ball, S.J. (2008) *The education debate* (Bristol, The Policy Press).
Beck, J. (2008) *Meritocracy, citizenship and education* (London, Continuum).
Belsky, J., Melhuish, E., Barnes, J., Leyland, A., Romaniuk, H. & the NESS Research Team (2006) Effects of Sure Start local programmes on children and families: early findings from a quasi-experimental, cross sectional study, *British Medical Journal,* 332, 1476–1478.
Bernstein, B. (1970) Education cannot compensate for society, *New Society,* 26 February.
Bhatti, G. (2000) *Asian children at home and at school* (London, Routledge).
Blair, T. (1998) *The Third Way: new politics for the new century.* Fabian Pamphlet 588 (London, The Fabian Society).
Blair, T. (2005) Speech on Education to *City of London Academy,* 12 September. Available online at 10 Downing Street website: http://www.pm.gov.uk/output/Page8181.asp (accessed 17 February 2008).
Blair, T. (2006) Speech at the *Specialist Schools and Academies Trust Conference 2006,* 30 November. Available online at 10 Downing Street website: http://www.pm.gov.uk/output/Page10514.asp (accessed 17 February 2008).
Blanden, J. & Machin, S. (2007) *Recent changes in intergenerational mobility in Britain.* Report for The Sutton Trust (Economics Department, University of Surrey and Centre for Economic Performance, London School of Economics).
Brantlinger, E. (2003) *Dividing classes: how the middle-class negotiates and rationalizes school advantage* (New York, RoutledgeFalmer).
Brown, G. (2006) We have renewed Britain, now we must champion it, *The Guardian,* 27 February, 15.
Brown, P. (1990) The 'third wave': education and the ideology of parentocracy, *British Journal of Sociology of Education,* 11(1) 65–85.
Buckingham, D. & Scanlon, M. (2003) *Education, entertainment and learning in the home* (Buckingham, Open University Press).
Burgess, S., Wilson, D. & Lupton, R (2005) Parallel lives? Ethnic segregation in England's schools and neighbourhoods, *Urban Studies,* 42(7), 1027–1056.
Chitty, C. (2007) Editorial: the Blair legacy, *FORUM: for promoting 3–19 comprehensive education,* 49(3), 203–206.
Crozier, G. (2000) *Parents and schools: partners or protagonists?* (Stoke on Trent, Trentham Books).
Crozier, G. (2005) Beyond the call of duty: the impact of racism on black parents' involvement in their children's education, in: G. Crozier & D. Reay (Eds) *Activating participation: parents and teachers working towards partnership* (Stoke on Trent, Trentham Books).
Crozier, G. & Reay, D. (2005) (Eds) *Activating participation: parents and teachers working towards partnership* (Stoke on Trent, Trentham Books).
David, M. E. (1993) *Parents, education and gender reform* (Cambridge, Polity Press).
DES (Department of Education and Science) (1985) *Better schools: a white paper* (London, HMSO).

DES (Department of Education and Science) (1988) *Education reform act* (London, HMSO).
DfEE (Department for Education and Employment) (1998) *Excellence in cities* (London, HMSO).
Dowling, T. (2008) The question: Are you an 'active citizen'? *The Guardian,* 24 January.
Edwards, A. & Warin, J. (1999) Parental involvement in raising the achievement of primary school pupils: why bother? *Oxford Review of Education,* 25(3), 325–341.
Gewirtz, S. (2001) 'Cloning the Blairs': New Labour's programme for the re-socialisation of working-class parents, *Journal of Education Policy,* 16, 365–378.
Gewirtz, S., Ball, S.J, & Bowe, R. (1995) *Markets, choice and equity* (Buckingham, Open University Press).
Gibbons, S., Machin, S. & Silva, O. (2006) *The educational impact of parental choice and school competition* (London, Centre for Economic Performance, London School of Economics).
Gillies, V. (2005) 'Raising the meritocracy': parenting and the individualisation of social class, *Sociology,* 39(5), 855–872.
Halsey, A. H. (1972) (Ed.) *Educational priority, vol 1: EPA problems and policies* (London, HMSO).
Hursh, D. (2004) Undermining democratic education in the USA: the consequences of global capitalism and neo-liberal policies for education policies at the local, state and federal levels, *Policy Futures in Education,* 2(3&4), 607–620.
Labour Party (1997) *New Labour because Britain deserves better* (London, The Labour Party Manifesto).
Labour Party (2005) *Britain forward not back* (London, The Labour Party Manifesto).
Machin, S. McNally, S. & Meghir, C. (2006) *Excellence in cities: evaluation of an education policy in disadvantaged areas.* Available online at: http://iserwww.essex.ac.uk/seminars/mondays/2006/spring/papers/mcnally.pdf (accessed 10 February 2008).
McCulloch, G. (1998) *Failing the ordinary child? The theory and practice of working-class secondary education* (Buckingham, Open University Press).
McNamara, O., Hustler, D., Stronach, I., Rodrigo, M., Beresford, E. & Botcherby, S. (2000) Room to manoeuvre: mobilising the 'active partner' in home–school relations, *British Educational Research Journal,* 26, 473–489.
Mulderrig, J. (2003) Consuming education: a critical discourse analysis of social actors in New Labour's education policy, *Journal for Critical Education Policy Studies,* 1(1).
Ofsted (Office for Standards in Education) (1994) *Reporting pupils' achievements* (London, HMSO).
Ofsted (Office for Standards in Education) (1995) *Guidance on the inspection of nursery and primary schools* (London, HMSO).
Reay, D. (1998) *Class work: mothers' involvement in their children's primary schooling* (London, University College Press).
Reay, D. (2006) The zombie stalking English schools: social class and educational inequality, *British Journal of Educational Studies* (Special issue on Social Justice), 54(3), 288–307.
Reay, D. (2008) Psycho-social aspects of white middle-class identities: desiring and defending against the class and ethnic 'other' in urban multiethnic schooling, *Sociology,* 42(6), 1072–1088.
Reay, D. & Ball, S. J. (1997) 'Spoilt for choice': the working-classes and education markets, *Oxford Review of Education,* 23(1), 89–101.
Reay, D. & Lucey, H. (2003). The limits of 'choice': children and inner city schooling, *Sociology,* 37, 121–142.
Reay, D., David, M. & Ball, S. J. (2005) *Degrees of choice* (Stoke on Trent, Trentham Books).
Reay, D., Hollingworth, S.K., Williams, Crozier, G., James, D., Jamieson, F. & Beedell, P. (2007) A darker shade of pale: whiteness, the middle-classes and multi-ethnic inner city schooling, *Sociology,* 41(6), 1041–1060.
Reynolds, D. & Cuttance, P. (1992) *School effectiveness: research, policy and practice* (London, Cassell).
Rose, N. (1999) *Powers of freedom: reframing political thought* (Cambridge, Cambridge University Press).

Russell, J. (2002) Pay as you learn, *The Guardian,* 8 April.

Scanlon, M. & Buckingham, D. (2004) Home learning and the educational marketplace, *Oxford Review of Education,* 30(2), 287–303.

Tomlinson, S. (2005) *Education in a post-welfare society* (2nd edn.) (Buckingham, Open University Press).

Townsend, M. (2003) Parents outspend schools on books, *The Observer,* 3 August, p. 8.

Vincent, C. (2000) *Including parents? Education, citizenship and parental agency* (Buckingham, Open University Press).

Vincent, C. & Ball, S. (2006) *Childcare choice and class practices: middle-class parents and their children* (London, Routledge).

Zero tolerance of failure and New Labour approaches to school improvement in England

Pam Sammons

Introduction

The emphasis on education highlighted by Tony Blair as his future Government's top priority involved a commitment to invest significant additional resources coupled with an explicit focus on accountability for the improvement of this key public service, including a promise to attack low standards in schools. In a previous special issue of the *Oxford Review of Education*, *Education and the Labour Government: an evaluation of two terms*, Walford (2005) highlighted the extent of change in almost every phase of education, while noting continuities with earlier Conservative approaches. However, while covering New Labour policies in relation to most major areas of education, the special issue did not address the role of 'zero tolerance of failure'.

Zero tolerance was a core principle across three terms of Blair's administration and remains influential under his successor Gordon Brown. Wide-ranging and cross-phase in its remit, the concern to identify and remedy perceived failure affected policies for all sectors. Its origins can be traced to an influential lecture ('The dark side of the moon: imagining an end to failure in urban education') made in 1995 by Michael Barber, a key New Labour education adviser. He claimed a serious debate about failure was necessary to challenge endemic low expectations and raise the quality of education in schools, especially those serving the disadvantaged. The approach, with its emphasis on combining pressure and support, has parallels with the 'tough on crime tough on the causes of crime' principle adopted by New Labour in relation to offending.

This paper examines New Labour's approaches to school improvement, particularly 'zero tolerance' strategies and their impact on school improvement, educational standards and equity and is informed by school effectiveness and improvement research perspectives.

Promoting good schools and eliminating failure

Standards and targets

The concept of standards is not used consistently by policy makers or academics. In England it can refer to absolute or relative levels of attainment in national assessment or public examination results, often in relation to 'expected' levels for a pupil age group at different Key Stages (KS). For example, the expected attainment in National Curriculum assessments in English, mathematics and science is Level 4 at KS2 (age 11), and five 'good' GCSE passes (%5A*–C) at KS4 (age 16). New Labour used these expectations as benchmarks to set increasingly ambitious attainment targets for pupils, schools and local education authorities (LEAs), including minimum 'floor' targets for poorly performing schools.

In the second and third terms contextual value added (CVA) indicators were developed to provide additional measures of school performance, based on school effectiveness research (SER) models. These take into account differences in pupil intake characteristics over which schools have little control, including prior attainment, social disadvantage measured by pupil eligibility for free school meals (FSM) and neighbourhood deprivation (Teddlie & Reynolds, 2000). However, the advent of CVA did not reduce the New Labour emphasis on simple benchmarks and attainment targets.

The Office for Standards in Education (Ofsted), England's national inspection agency, provided regular analysis and commentary on educational standards, quality of teaching and learning, leadership and school improvement through the HMCI annual report. This also examines the numbers and features of schools deemed to require special measures, in serious weaknesses or cause for concern (later termed 'notice to improve').

Different uses of the term standards, and the growing numbers of indicators, targets and different bases for judgments can cause confusion because schools classed as 'failing' in some measures may do well in others.

Diversity and centralisation: underlying tensions

New Labour sought to avoid ideological debates over grammar schools and selection, adopting a pragmatic approach and refusing to close popular schools with high standards. Instead it sought to make all schools 'good' schools, by raising overall standards through National Strategies, professional development, creating a National College for School Leadership (NCSL), an emphasis on inspection and investment and through promoting specialism and diversity. A drive to eliminate 'failing' schools through raising expectations, accountability and promoting improvement or, as a last resort, closure (often re-opening under new leadership and with new premises) was instituted.

The policy rhetoric was 'standards not structures' but in practice both were addressed. Some policies sought to target inequality and provide better opportunities for disadvantaged children (Excellence in Cities, Education Action Zones, Extended Schools, Children's Centres and pre-school expansion). Others, such as increased diversity, tended to act in an opposite direction (Chitty, 2004; Walford, 2005). Enhanced localisation and professionalism (more specialist schools, additional resources, improved pay and conditions, more freedom for successful schools, lighter touch inspection and increased self-evaluation) was evident alongside significantly enhanced centralisation (National Strategies, explicit standards and targets, reduced powers for Local Education Authorities (LEAs)).

Central control was viewed as especially important for the coordinated approach to remediate failing schools where the aim was intervention in inverse proportion to success (Barber, 2005). However, Whitty (2002) and Dyson and Raffo (2007) amongst others argued that the continued strength of social structure in accounting for educational inequality was too easily discounted by policy makers in the drive to hold schools to account for poor performance.

Taylor *et al.* (2005) suggested that policies promoting school diversity could exacerbate social inequity. The increase in diversity was intended to stimulate the 'modernisation' of comprehensive schools, and was linked to controversial solutions involving new forms of collaboration with Public–Private Partnerships (PPPs) taking over 'failing' LEAs and in new capital projects.

The emphasis on specialism and diversity was combined with new initiatives intended to support schools in challenging circumstances firstly via area-based initiatives such as Education Action Zones (EAZs), then Excellence in Cities (EiC) which was recognised as generally successful in improving pupil outcomes through new innovations such as the use of learning mentors and collaborative learning among staff. During the second term, a particular focus was given to improving secondary schools in the capital, where continued low standards caused political worries, leading to the high profile London Challenge (Matthews *et al.*, 2006). In addition, greater emphasis on combating educational disadvantage through multi-agency approaches and Extended Schools was evident (Dyson & Raffo, 2007).

Zero tolerance

SER originated with a concern to identify the features of effective schools often through studies of successful schools in low SES contexts, but increasingly during the 1990s the field focused on ineffective or failing schools (Reynolds, 1996). The links between effectiveness and school culture and context were increasingly recognised:

> A sinking school is a failing school. ... It is a school in which isolation, self-reliance, blame and loss of faith are dominating norms, and powerfully inhibit improvement. It will often, although not always, be in socially disadvantaged areas where parents are undemanding and teachers explain away failure by blaming inadequate parenting or unprepared children. (Stoll & Fink, 1998, p. 192)

Conservative education policy in the 1990s had increased accountability via regular Ofsted inspection and high stakes sanctions for poor performance to promote the 'withering away' of poor schools. Inspection was intended to identify weaknesses and schools required to take action to improve.

Ofsted became more powerful under New Labour with its role substantially widened to monitor and raise standards and tackle 'failure' across different sectors of education. Michael Barber, the first Head of the Standards and Effectiveness Unit (SEU), commented, 'On the issues of school failure and standards of literacy, the new labour critique was not that the [previous Conservative] government had been wrong to focus on them, but that it had not done enough to tackle them' (Barber, 2007, p. 9). The SEU prioritised more intense identification and remediation of failing schools.

The choice of academics from the school improvement and SER fields to head this Unit (Barber was followed by David Hopkins) reflects the importance attached to policy relevant research, and built on the approach adopted in the introduction of the National Literacy and Numeracy Strategies. Work on teacher effectiveness and failing schools was influential in shaping New Labour thinking (Reynolds, 1996; Hopkins *et al.*, 2005) while the concept of High Reliability Schools (Stringfield, 1995) informed school improvement strategies.

Zero tolerance of failure reflected both Blair's emphasis on aspirant parents and Blunkett's on promoting equity and counteracting professional vested interests (Barber, 2007). It led to the introduction of challenging national targets, concerted actions to identify any target failing and underperforming schools and, via area-based initiatives such as EAZ and EiC, more support for schools and communities in areas of greatest need.

'Naming and shaming'

Building on SER and inspection evidence it was argued that if some schools could gain good outcomes for disadvantaged groups this should be achieved by many more. The SEU argued that a history of blaming poverty and low expectations had led to acceptance of educational failure for large numbers of vulnerable pupils and that a cultural shift was needed at all levels of the education system (Barber, 2007). If a school could not be turned around quickly a radical new strategy was proposed, 'Fresh Start'. Barber had already been involved in the controversial closure of a failing school, Hackney Downs, in 1995. The stand taken on Hackney Downs became a foundation for New Labour's education policy, 'the high achieving Mossbourne Community Academy, standing on what was the site of Hackney Downs, is perhaps the most powerful symbol of Blair's legacy in education' (Barber, 2007, p. 26).

The symbolic intention of immediately identifying 'failing' schools for Fresh Start highlighted the new Government's commitment to putting pupils' educational entitlement first. The high profile placed enormous pressure and attention on Fresh Start schools, later seen as counter-productive owing to bad publicity (especially on behaviour) undermining improvement efforts in some schools, although most subsequently improved.

Many academics and professionals were strongly opposed to 'naming and shaming', zero tolerance and market solutions (Thrupp, 2002; Whitty, 2002; Power *et al.*, 2005). These were claimed to unfairly stigmatise staff working in the most challenging circumstances because it did not acknowledge the powerful impact of intake disadvantage and structural influences creating a cycle of poverty, poor parenting and family breakdown that educational research (Cox, 2000; Stevens, 2007) had shown to affect the life chances of disadvantaged children. Nonetheless, identification often acts as a major catalyst for improvement (Gray, 2000; Muijs *et al.*, 2004; Matthews & Sammons, 2005; Harris *et al.*, 2006, Ofsted, 2008).

The 'high challenge high support' performance management model with targeted interventions for schools failing to deliver was intended to address inequality and maintain confidence in the publicly funded education system, meet parents' higher expectations and reduce middle-class opt out to private schools (Barber 2005). The SEU drew on the teacher and SER and improvement knowledge base—and increasingly on inspection evidence—in developing approaches to work with schools, emphasised access to best practice and high quality professional development, good performance data and clear targets. Improvements in pay and conditions, attempts to raise professional esteem and additional support staff in schools, more resources and better buildings were intended to address problems of recruitment and retention to the profession and support the standards drive.

Research on schools improving in challenging contexts has drawn attention to the value of using data, target setting and professional development (Harris *et al.*, 2006). Gu *et al.* (2008) report that these strategies were viewed as particularly helpful by practitioners in schools that improved markedly over several years from a very low base.

Benchmarking and target setting have been criticised for creating a 'performativity' culture, narrowing the curriculum, inhibiting innovation and creativity in teaching and reducing pupils' enjoyment of school (Brooks & Tough, 2006). Policy initiatives such as Excellence and Enjoyment, Personalisation of Learning, Network Learning Communities and the Every Child Matters agenda represent attempts to reduce prescription, enhance informed professionalism and create a more equal partnership and better emotional climate between teachers and policy makers in the second term. Nonetheless, concerns remain about the continued policy emphasis on failure, accountability and standards (e.g. the Primary Review and Good Childhood Enquiry).

Improving poorly performing schools

Despite the greater emphasis on personalisation and flexibility in the second and third terms, the focus on failing/poor schools and teaching remained a consistent feature of education policy. Although the numbers of schools requiring special measures had fallen markedly, policy makers 'raised the bar' and widened their focus to include other low-attaining or under-performing schools (Figure 1) and more reliance was given to floor targets. Common problems in poorly performing schools noted by the independent National Audit Office (NAO, 2006) accord with those identified in SER (Gray, 2000; Muijs *et al.*, 2004). These include weak leadership or governance, unfilled staff vacancies, unfilled places, poor environment, poor standards of teaching and measures of pupil outcomes (high rates of absence, poor behaviour, low attainment), lack of external support and low parental engagement. Many of these can be seen as much as consequences as causes of poor performance.

The NAO's (2006) reference to the adverse impact of challenging circumstances as a feature of poorly performing schools and the link with educational disadvantage demonstrates the continued importance of context and intake. Similarly, Matthews and Sammons (2005) note that the risk of Ofsted special measures judgment was significantly higher for schools serving disadvantaged pupil intakes. Nonetheless, their data showed that despite the greater risk, most high disadvantage (FSM) schools

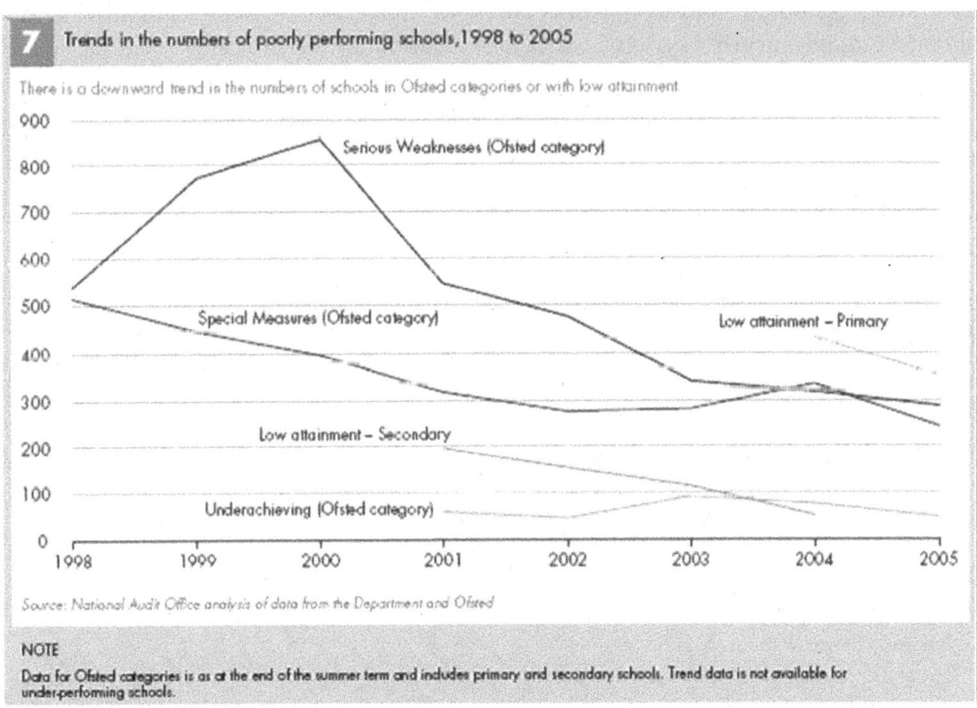

Figure 1. Trends in the numbers of different categories of 'poorly performing' schools 1998–2005 (NAO, 2006)

were not placed in special measures and numerically more special measures schools were located in advantaged areas.

Improvement through inspection

A large majority (85%) of schools placed in special measures recovered within two years and in most cases improvements were sustained (Matthews & Sammons, 2005; NAO, 2006). NAO (206) commended the role of high stakes inspection for identifying such weak schools and supported a return to more frequent, short notice inspection because of the adverse impact of poor education for pupils if left undetected for longer time periods. Comparisons of profiles for different categories of secondary schools show similarities in the time scale and trajectories to improved outcomes (Figures 1 and 2). Marked reductions in the numbers of schools placed in special measures and the less acute category of 'serious weaknesses' occurred under all three terms of New Labour. Although the numbers at any one time point are relatively low, over ten years the numbers of schools identified as in need of improvement that showed sustained improvement are sizeable. Matthews and Sammons (2005) argue that disadvantaged pupils are likely to have benefited in particular from such clear improvements in the quality of education because they tend to be over-represented in all categories of weak schools.

Ofsted (2008) examined how special measures schools sustain improvement and noted they benefited from strong leadership, set high expectations for pupil behaviour and developed effective systems for self-evaluation, while creating a strong school

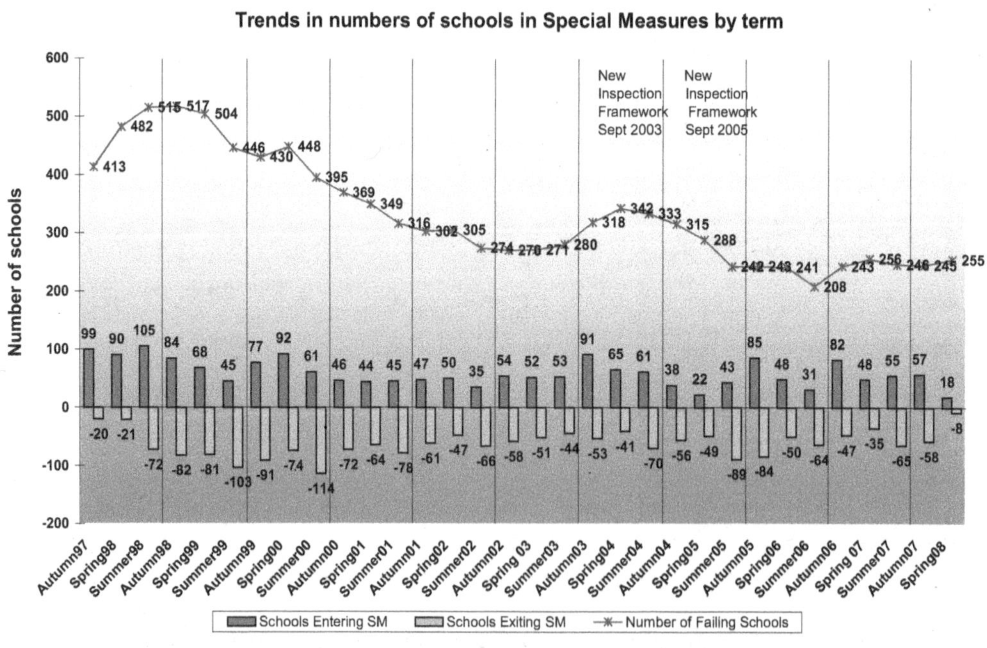

Figure 2. Numbers of schools in special measures 1997–2008 (source: DCSF)

identity that helped change the climate of failure. The importance of addressing pupil behaviour and school climate or culture echoes evidence from SER (Muijs *et al.*, 2004; Harris *et al.*, 2006; Reynolds *et al.*, 2006). It accords with conclusions from studies of ineffective schools that identified their lack of capacities to improve and of 'the organizational, social, cultural and symbolic "tightness" of the effective school' (Reynolds, 1996, p. 61). Such tightness appears to be a particularly important requirement for sustained improvement of schools in challenging contexts (Sammons *et al.*, 1997; Gray, 2000; Muijs *et al.*, 2004).

Fresh start and academies

Both Ofsted and NAO (2006) concluded that despite initial difficulties and bad publicity Fresh Start had been a success especially where LEAs, communities and pupils were consulted and involved. City Academies were viewed as engines of social justice initially intended to target failing secondary schools and provide radical new approaches to raise standards, especially for pupils and communities in disadvantaged areas. The Academies programme built on the Fresh Start experience and it was seen as a flagship policy much expanded in Blair's third term. The policy remains controversial due to the perceived lack of democratic accountability and emphasis on business and private sponsorship. Nonetheless, the NAO (2007) concluded Academies were popular, improved attainment levels and were likely to deliver good value for money. PricewaterhouseCoopers (2007) likewise noted variation at school level but overall improvements in comparisons with earlier predecessor schools. However, it is too early to evaluate the sustainability of such improvements.

The London and National Challenge

The London challenge was instituted in Labour's second term to address the high number of poorly performing secondary schools in the capital. It involved a wide range of support tailored to the needs of schools and drew on NCSL resources and accumulated evidence from school improvement and leadership research, professional and inspection evidence and other innovations, including EiC. Evaluations (Matthews *et al.*, 2006) suggest the London Challenge helped raise standards and target failure especially for lower performing schools and it was generally well received by professionals. The success led to an expansion to address primary schools and other areas (including Manchester) and it informed Brown's 2008 launch of the controversial National Challenge to eliminate poor school performance by 2011.

The National Challenge identified 638 secondary schools (performing under the 30% GCSE 5A*–C floor target) and committed £400 million. It was suggested that around a third could be closed and reopened as Academies or Trusts if they did not improve swiftly. The NUT strongly criticised the arbitrary approach and use of floor targets linked to raw results. Its own analysis indicated that a sizeable minority of these schools were not underperforming in CVA terms and in Ofsted inspection judgments. The emphasis on public identification remains a source of contention, with leaders of professional associations claiming that the major cause of poor performance is an unbalanced intake of pupils. Some head teachers argue that identification by the National Challenge can be counterproductive and may adversely affect pupil and staff recruitment.

Trends in attainment

Analyses of national assessment and examination data provide consistent evidence of improved overall levels of pupil attainment under New Labour. In the %5A*–C GCSE measure the upward trend was from 45.1% to 60.8% from 1997 to 2007. Using the more challenging GCSE measure including English and mathematics the improvement rate was from 35.6% to 46.0%. A higher rate of increase occurred in the most disadvantaged schools (defined by FSM bands) but may partly reflect the inclusion of GNVQ results or equivalent in the indicator. The floor target for secondary schools was raised in the third term from 25% to 30% including English and mathematics and on this basis 638 (21%) of secondary schools were below target. This represents a marked improvement on 1997 when over half (51%) of secondary schools had fewer than 30% of pupils achieving 5A*–C including English and mathematics (Figure 3).

Marked improvement in the attainments of primary pupils were associated with the introduction of the National Strategies and targeting of weak schools. By 2007 80% of pupils achieved Level 4+ for English at KS2 (up by 17% from 1997), 77% for mathematics (up 15%) and 88% for Science (up 19%). Nonetheless, the more challenging 85% target set for 2006 was missed and the failure of two in five pupils

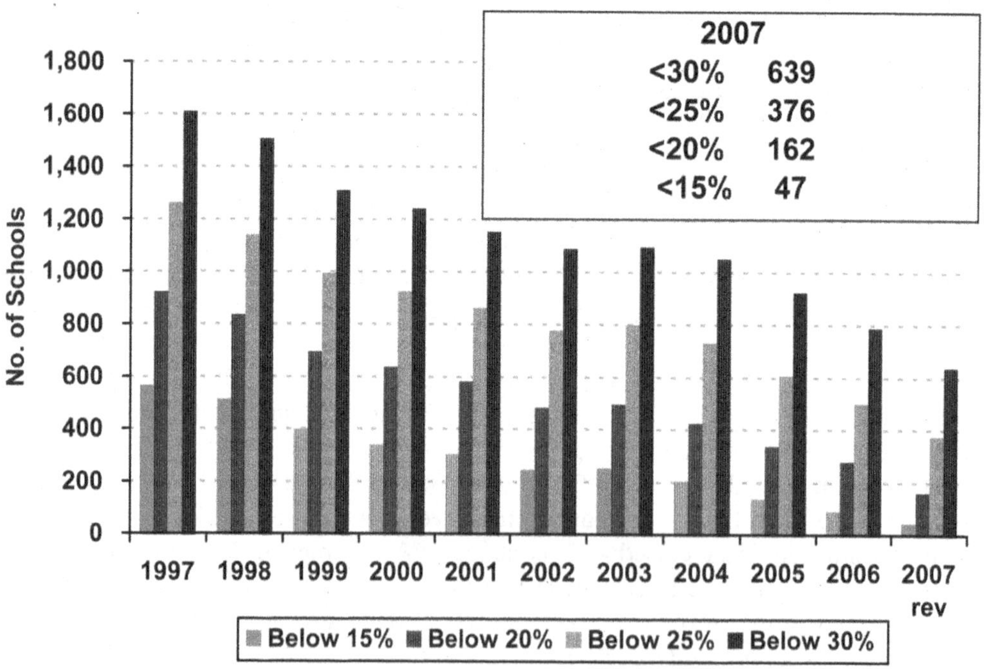

Figure 3. Numbers of low attaining secondary schools (%5A*–C GCSE including English and mathematics) 1997–2007 (source: DCSF)

to achieve Level 4 in both English and mathematics resulted in additional support programmes (Every Child a Reader and Every Child Counts).

Some argue that improvements in KS2 pupil attainment are largely illusory, reflecting teaching to the test and changes in national assessments (Tymms, 2004), although other evidence suggests real improvements have occurred (Massey *et al.*, 2003; Meadows *et al.*, 2007). In addition, international assessments (PIRLS, TIMSS) provide external evidence of increases in primary pupil attainment levels in England, especially in mathematics.

An analysis of teachers' views concluded:

> In general the Strategies were viewed very positively because they promoted continuity of teaching and learning in literacy and numeracy across all English schools, gave a structure and learning objectives for lessons, helped pupil understanding and provided ideas and resources for teachers. (Webb & Vulliamy, 2007, p. 568)

Nonetheless, the authors note teacher resentment of perceived Government prescription and lack of confidence in teachers' professional skills.

Ofsted's evaluation of the Strategies (2005) identified improved standards of attainment, teaching and pupil engagement, but concluded that in many schools the needs of low attaining pupils were not identified early enough to support them in closing the gap with their peers.

Narrowing the gap

The proportion of FSM pupils in the education system has fallen since 1997 and marked improvements in their absolute attainment levels are broadly in line with those of national trends, but the gap between disadvantaged pupil groups remains largely unchanged. New Labour strategies particularly linked with targets and zero tolerance of failure have supported a clear reduction in the gap in measured attainment between high and low performing schools on key indicators (National Statistics Office, 2006), and significant reductions in the absolute number of schools in special measures and those identified as poorly performing. However, approaches to reduce *relative* inequality (the size of the equity gap for vulnerable pupil groups such as white working class or black and some minority ethnic groups) have been much less successful (Bichard, 2007; Dyson & Raffo, 2007). This has been recognised during the third term with the creation of a Narrowing the Gaps Division in DCSF.

School improvement: New Labour's education legacy

Under Tony Blair education was seen as the public service best placed to combat social exclusion and improve life chances for vulnerable groups. Early years investment in families and pre-school was intended to give all children, but especially those most vulnerable, a better start at school and thus reduce the chances of later educational failure. Poorly performing and failing schools were seen to act against the equity emphasis because they often served more disadvantaged communities where improved aspirations and outcomes were deemed essential.

Despite some changes in tone, New Labour's education policy has consistently sought to promote higher standards, combat educational failure for schools and pupils, promote economic relevance and widen participation. The use of different indicators of performance (floor targets based on 'raw' results, CVA and inspection judgments), however, can create confusion where some schools appear sound in one measure but not in others. CVA is now widely recognised as a fairer performance measure for schools than raw results. However, pupils' actual attainment levels have a great significance for their future educational and employment prospects, therefore they are relevant in investigating the extent that policy change is able to narrow the equity gap.

Blair's education legacy includes significant and sustained improvements in overall pupil attainment levels and for the majority of schools in many aspects of quality (including teaching and leadership, equipment and buildings). Whether the major extra resourcing in terms of proportion of GDP will be sustained longer term if there is a change of Government and economic outlook remains questionable. There has been considerable success in reducing the numbers of schools identified as requiring special measures or in the categories 'serious weaknesses'/'notice to improve', and those poorly performing. Continuity with past Conservative policies on accountability coupled with greater investment, professional development and major initiatives such as the National Strategies, combined pressure and support. High profile initiatives such as Fresh Start and the Academies programme were small in scale (though expanding) but promoted change even in schools with a long history of problems. More flexibility and freedom were encouraged for the majority of schools but not those identified as weak. Here evidence from SER and improvement studies (that many such schools lacked the leadership and capacities to improve without external intervention to promote organisational and cultural change) led to the strategy of intervention in inverse proportion to success.

Reductions in the number of 'failing' schools and those with poor performance have occurred despite a more challenging inspection framework intended to 'raise the bar' and more frequent inspection, coupled with higher floor targets. Some have suggested that the identification of schools as failing leads to a 'spiral' of decline but the results for special measures schools, Fresh Start and Academies reveal improvements in attainment, climate and quality of provision in most cases. Much has been learnt about improvement strategies from programmes such as EiC and the London Challenge and the role of contextual sensitivity and tailored strategies (Muijs *et al.*, 2004; Harris *et al.*, 2006; Reynolds *et al.*, 2006) and about the processes, problems and possibilities of national education reform (Hopkins *et al.*, 2005). These policy emphases and changes have proved unpopular with many academics and professionals, however, with concerns about performativity, prescription, de-professionalism, PPP and controversy over the role of specialist schools and Academies and may lead to changes in emphasis in future administrations.

The legacy on promoting equity in outcomes for pupils is more questionable. Despite rising attainment levels and widening of participation, there has been little narrowing of longstanding and sizeable attainment gaps. Those from disadvantaged backgrounds remain at higher risk of poor outcomes at all stages. Blair's education policies have had only modest success in combating social exclusion, though investment in early years may yet show longer term benefits. Nonetheless, disadvantaged groups are likely to have benefited from the improvements in schools' educational facilities and quality of teaching and learning under New Labour, especially if they attended one of the many turn around schools previously identified as special measures, in serious weakness or poorly performing, and from extra investments in disadvantaged areas through programmes such as Sure Start, EiC and Extended Schools.

Comparative case studies of successful school systems comment on the importance of monitoring, feedback and the role of independent professional agencies to conduct evaluation and identify schools that need intervention and support (Dobert & Sroka, 2004). This accords with the 'pressure and support' model used in England and part of the Blair education legacy can be seen in the international impact on other systems' approaches to school improvement.

Improvements over the last decade are to be welcomed but it is clear that the extent to which schools can overcome the effects of social disadvantage remain limited (Harris *et al.*, 2006; Dyson & Raffo, 2007). Nonetheless, their potential to ameliorate its effects and enhance the life chances and outcomes of disadvantaged pupils is important and the aspect most open to intervention (Mortimore, 1995; Sammons, 2007). Attending a school identified as academically more effective is particularly relevant for disadvantaged pupil groups because attending a poor school compounds existing disadvantage while an effective school helps reduce its adverse impact (Scheerens & Bosker, 1997; Cox, 2000, Sammons *et al.*, 2007; Stevens, 2007). Sustained reductions in the numbers of schools identified as weak or failing therefore remains a substantive legacy.

References

Barber, M. (1995) The dark side of the moon: imagining an end to failure in urban education, *The TES/Greenwich Education Lecture.*

Barber, M. (2005) Journeys of discovery the search for success by design, Keynote Speech *National Centre for Education and the Economy Annual Conference,* Florida, 10 February.

Barber, M. (2007) *Instruction to deliver Tony Blair, public services and the challenge of achieving targets* (London, Politico's Publishing).

Bichard, M. (2007) (Ed.) *Challenging educational disadvantage* (London, SOLACE Foundation Imprint).

Brooks, R. & Tough, S. (2006) *Assessment and teaching: making space for teaching and learning* (London, Institute of Public Policy Research).

Chitty, C. (2004) *Education policy in Britain* (Basingstoke, Palgrave Macmillan).

Cox, T. (Ed.) (2000) *Combating educational disadvantage: meeting the needs of vulnerable children* (London, Falmer Press).

Dobert, H. & Sroka, W. (2004) *Features of successful school systems, a comparison of schooling in six countries* (Munster, Waxmann).

Dyson, A. & Raffo, C. (2007) Education and disadvantage: the role of community-oriented schools, *Oxford Review of Education,* 33(3), 297–314.

Gray, J. (2000) *Causing concern but improving: a review of schools' experiences on special measures* (London, Department for Education and Employment Research Series).

Gu, Q., Sammons, P. & Mehta, P. (2008) Leadership characteristics and practices in schools with different effectiveness and improvement trajectories, *School Leadership and Management,* 28(1), 43–63.

Harris, A., Chapman, C., Muijs, D., Russ, J. & Stoll, L. (2006) Improving schools in challenging contexts: exploring the possible, *School Effectiveness and School Improvement,* 17(4), 409–424.

Hopkins, D., Reynolds, D. & Gray, J. (2005) *School improvement lessons from research* (London, DfES).

Massey, A., Green, S., Dexter, T. & Hamnett, L. (2003) *Comparability of national tests over time: KS1, KS2 and KS3 standards between 1996 and 2001, Final Report to QCA of the Comparability Over Time Project* (Cambridge, UCLES).

Matthews, P. & Sammons, P. (2005) Survival of the weakest: the differential improvement of schools causing concern in England, *London Review of Education,* 3(2), 159–176.

Matthews, P., Sammons, P., Gu, Q. & Day, C. (2006) *Supporting leadership and securing quality, an evaluation of the impact of aspects of the London Leadership Strategy,* Report for the NCSL (Nottingham, School of Education University of Nottingham/NCSL).

Meadows, S., Herrick, D., Feiler, A. & the ALSPAC Study Team (2007) Improvements in national test reading scores at Key Stage 1; grade inflation or better achievement?, *British Educational Research Journal,* 33(1), 47–59.

Mortimore, P. (1995) The positive effects of schooling, in: M. Rutter (Ed.) *Psycho-social disturbance in young people: challenges for prevention* (Cambridge: Cambridge University Press).

Muijs, D. & Reynolds, D. (2005) *Effective teaching* (London, Paul Chapman).

Muijs, D., Harris, A., Chapman, C., Stoll, L. & Russ, J. (2004) Improving schools in socio-economically disadvantaged areas: a review of research evidence, *School Effectiveness and School Improvement,* 15(2), 149–172.

NAO (National Audit Office) (2006) *Improving poorly performing schools in England* (London, National Audit Office/DfES).

NAO (National Audit Office) (2007) *The academies programme* (London, The Stationery Office).

National Statistics Office (2006) *Statistics of education trends in attainment gaps: 2005* (London, DfES).

Power, S., Rees, G. & Taylor, C. (2005) New Labour and educational disadvantage: the limits of area based interventions, *London Review of Education,* 3(2), 101–116.

Ofsted (Office for Standards in Education) (2005) *The Primary National Strategy: an evaluation of its impact in primary schools 2004/05* (London, Ofsted).

Ofsted (Office for Standards in Education) (2008) *Sustaining improvement: the journey from special measures* (London, Ofsted).

PricewaterhouseCoopers (2007) *Academies evaluation 4th annual report* (London, DCSF).

Reynolds, D. (1996) Turning around ineffective schools: some evidence and some speculation, in: J. Gray, D. Reynolds, C. Fitz-Gibbon & D. Jesson (Eds) *Merging traditions: the future of research on school effectiveness and improvement* (London, Cassell).

Reynolds, D. (2005) How can recent research in school effectiveness, teacher effectiveness and school improvement inform our thinking about educational policies? In D. Hopkins, D. Reynolds & J. Gray, (Eds) *School improvement lessons from research* (London, DfES).

Reynolds, D., Harris, A., Clarke, P., Harris, B. & James, S. (2006) Challenging the challenged: developing an improvement programme for schools facing exceptionally challenging circumstances, *School Effectiveness and School Improvement,* 17(4), 425–440.

Sammons, P. (2007) *School effectiveness and equity: making connections* (Reading, CfBT).

Sammons, P., Thomas, S. & Mortimore, P. (1997) *Forging links: effective schools and effective departments* (London, Paul Chapman).

Sammons, P., Sylva, K., Melhuish, E., Siraj-Blatchford, I., Taggart, B. & Grabbe, Y. (2007) *Influences on children's attainment and progress in Key Stage 2: cognitive outcomes in Year 5.* DCSF Research Report No. RR828 (Nottingham, DCSF Publications).

Scheerens, J. & Bosker, R. (1997) *The foundations of educational effectiveness* (Oxford, Pergamon).

Stevens, P. (2007) Researching race/ethnicity and educational inequality in English secondary schools: a critical review of the literature between 1980 and 2005, *Review of Educational Research,* 7(2), 147–185.

Stoll, L. & Fink, D. (1998) The cruising school: the unidentified ineffective school, in: L. Stoll & K. Myers (Eds) *No quick fixes: perspectives on schools in difficulty* (London, Falmer Press).

Stringfield, S. (1995) Attempting to improve students' learning through innovative programs—the case for schools evolving into high reliability organisations, *School Effectiveness and School Improvement,* 6(1), 67–96.

Taylor, C., Fitz, J. & Gorard, S. (2005) Diversity, specialism and equity in education, *Oxford Review of Education,* 31(1), 47–69.

Teddlie C. & Reynolds, D. (2000) *The international handbook of school effectiveness research* (Lewes, Falmer Press).

Thrupp, M. (2002) Why 'meddling' is necessary: a response to Teddlie, Reynolds, Townsend, Scheerens, Bosker & Creemers, *School Effectiveness and School Improvement,* 13(1), 1–14.

Tymms, P. (2004) Are standards rising in British primary schools? *British Educational Research Journal,* 30(4), 477–494.

Walford, G. (2005) Introduction: education and the Labour Government, *Oxford Review of Education,* 31(1), 3–9.

Webb, R. & Vulliamy, G. (2007) Changing classroom practice at Key Stage 2: the impact of New Labour's national strategies, *Oxford Review of Education,* 33(5), 561–580.

Whitty, G. (2002) *Making sense of education policy* (London, Paul Chapman).

Academies and diplomas: two strategies for shaping the future workforce

Richard Hatcher

Introduction

The most fundamental legacy of the Blair government in school education in England is to have established the production of 'human capital' for the competitiveness of the British economy as the master narrative of policy. In Tony Blair's words:

> Education is our best economic policy ... This country will succeed or fail on the basis of how it changes itself and gears up to this new economy, based on knowledge. Education is now the centre of economic policy making for the future. (Blair, 2005)

Gordon Brown's first speech on education as leader of the Labour Party, on 20 June 2007, to an audience from the City of London, established the continuity of policy. Its theme was the centrality of education to Britain's economic competitiveness. 'It is investment in education that when combined with free trade, open markets and flexibility makes for the virtuous circle of an inclusive globalisation' (Brown, 2007).

The dominance of the economic function of education is not unique to New Labour: it was first signalled by James Callaghan in 1976. The succeeding Thatcher government put in place two key strategies, marketisation and state regulation, but its ability to drive through the modernising project was hindered by the conflicting pressures of cultural restorationists and anti-statist free-marketeers. Nor is it unique to Britain: the Lisbon Declaration of 2000 marked the harnessing of education to the economic objectives of the European Union (EU). What is distinctive about New Labour has been its ability, taking advantage of the defeat of trade union resistance by the Thatcher government, to pursue the modernising project by adopting a much more interventionist state strategy than either its predecessor or other European governments, employing the full repertoire of strategies provided by the 'New Public Management'.

> The OECD's Public Management Service has claimed that 'a new paradigm for public management has emerged, aimed a fostering a performance-orientated culture in a less centralised public sector' (OECD, 1995, p. 8). The term 'new public management' (NPM) ... centres on corporatisation and commercialisation, privatisation, competition and contracting, deregulation and liberalisation, performance management and restructuring the financing of public services. (Whitfield, 2001, p. 114)

The boundaries between the public and the private, the state and the market, government and business, have been radically blurred and redrawn, creating a new and complex educational landscape. The private sector is a key agent of transformation of the school system at every level, from the implementation, and formation, of national policy initiatives to the provision of outsourced Local Authority services and 'school improvement' solutions to schools (Hatcher, 2006; Ball, 2007).

For roughly the first half of the Blair government's period of office the dominant theme was the 'standards agenda'. The rationale was that a general improvement in pupil attainment through 'school improvement' would be the principal means of furnishing the labour power potential which the economy was deemed to need. Test scores steadily improved. Criticisms of the 'standards agenda' could be rebutted with evidence that it worked. But during Blair's second term of office it became apparent that the rise in attainment had levelled off, that much of it was due to teachers teaching to the test, and that the equality gap remained wide (see, for example, Tymms *et al.*, 2005). Influential education advisers to government warned that 'what looks like apparent success in turning around schools is actually quite superficial and indeed illusory' (Fullan, 2005, p. 1) and spoke of 'the failure of performance based reform' (Hopkins, 2007, p. 24).

Meanwhile, the EU produced a series of reports warning that far from achieving the Lisbon goals the productivity of the European economy continued to lag behind that of the United States and was increasingly vulnerable to competition from China and India (Jones *et al.*, 2008). In England employers' continuing complaints about the skills of new entrants to the workforce were endorsed by the Leitch Report (Leitch, 2006), warning that the UK was 'on track to achieve undistinguished mediocrity' if it fails to upgrade the skills of its workforce by 2020.

This marked a crisis in Labour's education project and a turning point in policy. The focus on a general rise in pupil attainment was insufficient to satisfy 'human capital' requirements. It needed to be accompanied by the direct and targeted involvement of employers in the formation of the future workforce. To this end the Blair government developed two linked strategies. One is to involve business interests directly in the curriculum in the form of new vocationally-oriented courses and qualifications designed under the auspices of employer-led Diploma Development Partnerships. Again, this is not unique to Britain (or rather, England, because by now education policy in the four countries of the UK had significantly diverged). The development of more distinct 'academic' and vocationally-oriented pathways in secondary education is occurring in other countries in Europe such as France and Italy.

The other strategy is to enable business interests—individuals and companies—to run state schools, as sponsors of Academies and Trusts. There is no direct parallel in other Western European countries, though there is evidence of policy influence from state schools run by private sector organisations in Sweden and the United States. These two strategies partly overlap in the form of vocationally-oriented Academies sponsored by local employers and geared to local labour market needs.

Both strategies remain key policies of the Brown government and have been endorsed by the Conservative opposition. However, whether these two strategies can provide the basis of a stable policy settlement depends decisively upon the extent to which they prove capable of delivering a more economically competitive future workforce.

The new 14–19 agenda

In 2005 the government's *14–19 Education and Skills White Paper* (DfES, 2005) announced a new agenda for 14–19 education which was intended to achieve 'the long-term transformation of vocational education in support of a high productivity, flexible economy' (p. 11). Alan Johnson, the then Education Secretary, described it as 'the most radical educational development taking place probably anywhere in the world' (Webster & Frean, 2006).The centre-piece of the reform is the creation of 17 courses leading to a new qualification, a Diploma, at three levels. Fourteen of these diploma courses are each based on a particular industry sector. Pilots in five vocational sectors start in September 2008, with all the diplomas available by 2013.

The 14–19 agenda creates three tracks at Key Stage 4: an 'academic' track following the traditional GCSE route to A levels; a new broad middle stream, the diplomas, which can include GCSE courses; and a smaller bottom stream of work-related learning leading to a Modern Apprenticeship. It represents the formal abandonment of the idea of a common national curriculum till 16 which was embodied in the 1988 Education Reform Act, but it consolidates the practice of many schools, at least since the review of the National Curriculum in 2000, of operating vocationally-oriented pathways for 'non-academic' pupils (Jephcote & Abbott, 2005).

The 14–19 agenda combines an educational and an economic rationale: that a more practical and work-related curriculum at Key Stage 4 is capable both of meeting the skill needs of employers and of motivating young people and enabling them to succeed in ways which the traditional academic curriculum can not.

There are two other anticipated benefits for government of diplomas compared to the existing 'academic' curriculum. One is that there are insufficient jobs in the youth labour market to assimilate school leavers, and diplomas, with their combination of a more practical curriculum and the promise of employment advantage, may be more effective in keeping lower-achieving and 'disaffected' young people in education until 18 (Allen & Ainley, 2007). The other is that their favourable equivalence tariff with GCSEs and A levels will enable government to claim the continuing success of its education policy in raising standards of attainment. There may also be electoral benefits if middle-class parents perceive the diplomas to be reinforcing social segregation within and between schools to their advantage.

The implementation of the 14–19 agenda

Critics have pointed to a number of problems with the implementation of the new diplomas. First, will pupils choose the diploma courses rather than the GCSE and A level route with which the diplomas are in competition (though diplomas can include GCSEs and A levels within them)? Second, no school will be able to offer more than one or two diplomas. Will students travel to other institutions? Third, will schools and colleges collaborate effectively to provide the full range of diplomas in each local area when at the same time they are in competition with each other to attract students and achieve results (Hodgson & Spours, 2007)?

But these problems of implementation are not decisive. The fundamental issue is: will the diplomas provide a long-term solution to the human capital problem? The answer depends upon two further questions: what is the content of the diplomas and are they what employers want?

Diplomas, local authorities and local labour markets

There is an ongoing debate about the nature of the proposed diplomas, centring on the degree to which they will be more general or more narrowly vocational. The House of Commons Education and Skills Committee remarked that 'It has not always been clear to what extent the new programmes are intended to be vocational, or applied, or to serve a more general purpose' (House of Commons Education and Skills Committee, 2007, p. 13). The Nuffield Review *Issues paper 1: The New 14–19 Diplomas* (Hodgson *et al.*, 2007) refers to the original 14 diplomas as a middle-track vocational pathway, but an appended response by Graham Lane and the 14 diploma Chairs rejects this characterisation. However, local authorities, responsible for managing the setting up of local area partnerships, are in no doubt that the diplomas are vocational, and that this is their distinctive value for simultaneously meeting the educational needs of lower-achieving students and equipping them with the skills which are required by the local economy. To give one typical example, Sunderland claims that its programme will 'break the cycle of underachievement *by close alignment of the curriculum to future high value added employment needs*' in three job sectors—health and social care, business and financial services, and automotive (City of Sunderland, 2005, p. 113, emphasis in original).

While there are undoubtedly labour market skill needs in specific sectors in specific local areas, that does not guarantee that there will be a vacancy for every school leaver with a related diploma (particularly in a period of economic downturn), or that there is a match between the skills acquired in the diploma courses and those required in the workplace. In an analysis of national labour market trends Jon Cruddas (2006) notes a growing polarisation within the labour market:

> On the one hand, a primary labour market—or the knowledge-based economy—covering about 21 per cent of jobs. On the other hand an expanding secondary labour market where the largest growth is occurring—in service-related elementary occupations, administrative and clerical occupations, sales occupations, caring personal service occupations and the like. (Cruddas, 2006, pp. 37–38)

The polarisation of the labour market has profound implications for the government's vocational agenda. The traditional academic route of GCSEs and A levels will continue to supply entrants to the professional, managerial and higher technical sectors. The destiny of the majority of diploma holders will be not the knowledge economy which the government promises but the expanding secondary labour market. The question then is what currency will diplomas have with employers in that sector?

The employers' view is summed up by a managing director quoted in the latest Confederation of British Industry's *Education & Skills Survey 2008* (CBI, 2008):

> We believe firmly that the educational system should produce reliable basic material on which employers can build at their own expense to provide vocational skills. (CBI, 2008, p. 14. See also Martin *et al.*, 2008)

A significant number of jobs in the secondary labour market do not require qualifications at all. Ewart Keep (2005) argues that:

> ... the patchy and possibly declining salience of qualifications (particularly below degree level) in the recruitment and selection process across large swathes of the labour market has been steadfastly ignored by policy-makers and those who manage the VET system. (p. 543)

Keep's explanation is a shift in employers' requirements from 'hard' to 'soft' skills (OECD, 2002). On this basis there is an apparent mismatch between the specific occupationally-oriented skills which diplomas certify, which are irrelevant for many employers, and the generalised soft skills and personal attributes these employers look for, which the diplomas do not explicitly certify. But the mismatch is only apparent. The real focus of the diploma policy is not on 'hard' skills and occupation-related knowledge but on the formation of new subjectivities. In Bourdieu's terms, the diploma programme is a field designed to construct the habitus of the new future worker's identity-in-formation. The doxa of this ideal emerging vocational identity comprises a relationship to employment and a relationship to knowledge. The former foregrounds dispositions: flexibility, adaptability, entrepreneurialism, a compliant creativity, a willingness to take responsibility for their own 'employability'. Underpinning it is a different relationship to knowledge from that of the 'academic' curriculum, one in which knowledge is 'stripped of universal pretensions, becoming localised and tied to the enactment of skill in the workplace' (Avis, 2002). In this perspective the function of diploma courses is the formation of generalised labour power potential. Their occupational specificity furnishes the surface content, but the intended deep learning is the formation of new generalised class-based subjectivities attuned to what James Avis calls the 'performative logic' of the labour market.

The extent to which diploma courses at Key Stage 4 succeed in this function depends first on how many students, and schools, choose the diploma route and how convincingly it is perceived by students to relate to the workplace. While a more practical work-related course may prove more attractive to students than the 'academic' curriculum (as evidence from the Increased Flexibility Programme suggests; Higham & Yeomans, 2006), the indications so far of tenuous links with employers, largely classroom-based teaching with only ten days required work experience, and lack of credible resources and staffing raise doubts about the diplomas (Allen, 2007). In addition, the attraction of diplomas will be undermined if future feedback about their labour market currency is negative, though some students may use them instead for access to the lower echelons of higher education, increasing the pressure on diplomas of 'academic drift' (Allen & Ainley, 2007).

Academies, employers and the labour market

I turn now to the government's second strategy to stimulate the more efficient production of human capital in the school system by directly involving the private sector. Academies are state schools run by 'sponsors' who form a majority of the governing body and thereby control the curriculum, admissions and staffing. This provides the opportunity for business interests, whether individual business people, companies, or other types of business organisations (such as charitable trusts), to directly shape the future workforce.

Certainly this is the aim of a number of local authorities. For example, Nottingham's *Building Schools for the Future—Strategic Business Case* (Nottingham City Council, 2006, p. 83) says, 'By careful links with the local business community, it is anticipated that the specialism of each Academy can be linked with local workforce demand and address key skills shortages'. The most developed example is Manchester, where the local authority is brokering the establishment of six Academies with this purpose (Manchester City Council, 2006).

However, only a small minority of Academies are sponsored by companies. The 83 Academies open prior to September 2008 have 105 sponsors, of which 11 are companies. The Academies at the feasibility stage have nine company sponsors out of 99 sponsors, and at the implementation stage have four out of 26. The total is 24 companies out of 230 sponsors, representing a stable trend over time of approximately 10%.

In addition there are individual business men and women sponsors. Of the 83 Academies open prior to September 2008, 16 have sponsors in this category. But of the 74 in the feasibility stage, only four have sponsors in this category. It appears that the government was able to involve individual multimillionaire businessmen in the first wave of Academies, but that this pool is drying up.

The overall picture is of only limited involvement by companies and business entrepreneurs in sponsoring Academies. It is striking that the CBI's *Education and Skills Survey 2008* (CBI, 2008) makes no mention at all of Academies, except by implication in the concluding negative comment that:

> There is a strong demand from many schools to develop links with business, but feedback from CBI members indicates too many schools just see businesses as a source for sponsorship and businesses find the plethora of existing initiatives too complex. (p. 49)

In this respect the Academies seem likely to be repeating the failure of their forerunners, the Conservative government's City Technology Colleges. Some CTCs were sponsored by local businesses but the programme remained small because of lack of interest by companies (Ball, 2008).

Will Academies solve the problems of inadequate basic skills which employers complain about? The government claims that Academies are more effective than normal schools in raising standards of attainment in socially disadvantaged areas. However, the evidence from the annual evaluations of Academies which the government commissions from PricewaterhouseCoopers does not bear this claim out. According to the most recent report Academies performed no better than similar schools which were not Academies (PricewaterhouseCoopers, 2007, p. 36).

> ...across the 21 Academies that were open in 2006, 40 per cent of pupils achieved Key Stage 4 Level 2 (5+ A*-C) ... When compared to other similar schools, the level of performance in Academies in 2006 was similar to the two comparison groups (both 41 per cent compared to the Academy average of 40 per cent)...

It is also claimed that students make more progress in Academies than in comparable schools. Again, the evidence from the PWC evaluation does not support this claim. Of the eight Academies open in 2003, the average increase over three years in the percentage of pupils gaining five A*–C grades was 13%, compared to almost identical figures in the two Comparison Groups schools of 12% and 13%.

Government claims for the success of Academies have rested largely on their use of GNVQs as the equivalent of four grade C GCSEs and no stipulation of GCSE passes in English and mathematics. The introduction of the latter criteria shows Academies eight percentage points higher in 2006 than the schools they replaced in 2002. However, since all schools nationally had improved by an average four percentage points, the actual relative 'value-added' amounts to four percentage points, which is accountable largely if not entirely by the substantial change in social class composition of many Academies, as measured by the reduction in pupils entitled to free school meals. Particularly important, in view of employers' complaints about the basic skills of school-leavers, is the attainment of lower-achieving pupils. The most basic success criteria at age 16 is Level 1, i.e. five or more A*–G grades. Nationally in 2006 19% of pupils in Academies did not achieve this level, which is slightly worse than their predecessor schools. The situation improved in 2007, but again the main factors are changing social composition (Anti-Academies Alliance, 2008).

Of course, these figures do not distinguish between business-run Academies and others. It is conceivable that the former are relatively more effective, but there is no evidence available that they might be.

Finally, is it the case that business-run Academies furnish particularly effective fields for the formation of a pro-business habitus in their students, imbuing them with business values and attitudes? According to PricewaterhouseCoopers (2005, p. 13), 'The evidence shows that the vision is set and defined by the sponsor, and then operationalised by the principal'. 'Business and enterprise' is by far the most popular choice of specialism of sponsors from the world of business, accounting for 22 of the Academies open at the time of writing. However, there is no research evidence available as yet of the impact of business sponsorship of Academies on the emerging vocational identities of their students, including whether a general pro-business ethos is effective or whether a more organic integration of the Academy with the world of work is necessary to secure the formation of appropriate labour power potential.

The private sector and the formation of the future workforce

I have argued that the failure of the 'standards agenda' to achieve the improvements in attainment that the government regards as necessary for producing the human capital required for the competitiveness of the British economy has provoked a new phase of New Labour education policy. Its principal theme is a closer engagement of employers with schools, to be accomplished through two overlapping strategies: a new vocationally-oriented track in the school curriculum, and business interests controlling schools as sponsors of Academies (and potentially Trust schools as well). Will they provide the basis of a successful new policy settlement?

In the case of Academies, the evidence so far raises serious doubts. A number of local authorities are attempting to broker Academies linked to local labour markets, but the trend is of relatively few Academies attracting employers as sponsors, and not all of them have a local vocational orientation. In any case, the impact of business sponsors on students' vocational identities is unclear. It seems likely, given their social composition, that the large majority of Academies will deliver diploma programmes, but with companies as 'partners' rather than sponsors. In this respect they will be no different from other schools serving predominantly working-class areas. Nor, if present trends continue, are Academies likely to be any more successful than comparable non-Academy schools in raising pupil attainment.

How diplomas will work in practice remains to be seen. Local partnership provision may well be constrained by a combination of delivery problems and student preference for remaining at their own school. For some students they will provide both skills and qualifications which employers seek. But for many, in the context of current labour market predictions concerning future employment in the low-skill sectors of the economy, specific occupationally-related qualifications will have little purchase, except insofar as employers use them as a general recruitment filter (Allen & Ainley, 2007). Whether the diplomas are more successful in providing the soft skills and employable dispositions, as well as the core skills, which employers require remains to be seen, though the shaping of the emerging vocational identities of school-students to fit the neo-liberal economy would seem to depend on a closer integration of the classroom and the workplace than most schools are likely to be able to offer and most employers seem interested in investing in.

In short, Blair has bequeathed to his successors two major reforms in the school system which seem unlikely to resolve the fundamental problem of supplying the workforce it is claimed that capital requires and thereby providing the basis for a durable policy settlement. It is very possible that by 2010 Labour will be replaced by a Conservative government, itself the legacy of New Labour. The Conservatives have stated their support for both the diploma programme and Academies. Nick Gibb, the shadow schools minister, has said, 'We want the new vocational diplomas to work so that there is a high quality alternative for those children that don't want to study academic qualifications' (Gibb, 2008). David Willetts, Shadow Secretary of State for Innovation, Universities and Skills, has stated:

> We can use the academy programme far more ambitiously to tackle supply side problems that have stood in the way of real school reform in this country. We will not just stand behind the Academies already created, we will push Tony Blair's Academies Programme further and faster. (Willetts, 2007)

However, the most recent substantive Conservative Party policy document on education, *Raising the bar, closing the gap* (Conservative Party, 2007) makes no mention at all of diplomas in its 52 pages, and while it champions Academies in terms of offering parents choice, it does not refer at all to their having a vocational function. In fact, its ideal candidates as sponsors are specified as the United Learning Trust, the Oasis Trust, the Woodard Trust, and the City Livery Companies—the first three are Anglican organisations, only the last has any sort of business connection.

It is possible to sketch out a number of possible post-election policy scenarios for the school system, in a period of continuing economic downturn and intensified global competition, with varying permutations of diploma and Academy trajectories. In the first, direct business involvement in diplomas significantly increases. The system becomes increasingly segregated at Key Stage 4 into academic and vocational streams. Diplomas diverge from GCSEs and become entirely work-related programmes, often in FE colleges or with private providers, and with longer periods of workplace experience. The learning situation becomes more like a workplace, drawing on the 'studio school' model.

In the second scenario employers continue to complain about new entrants to the workforce but show no increased interest in becoming involved in diploma courses. They remain classroom-based with minimal workplace experience. The history of previous attempts to link school and work more closely is repeated (e.g. Esland, 1996), though with two possible variants. In one, the academic-vocational boundary hardens into two segregated and social class-based streams; in the other, they become assimilated into a mixed (though still socially differentiated) academic/vocational economy of provision.

Another set of possibilities concerns business sponsorship of schools in working-class areas. One scenario is of employers as sponsors running Academies and Trusts and gearing them to local labour market needs. Another is of the spread of branded chains of Academies, some on for-profit management contracts, rivalling local authorities in scope, but with, as today, only a minority run by employers. There are parallels with some American cities—Philadelphia (Bulkley, 2007), Chicago (Lipman & Hursh, 2007, Means, 2008).

The factors determining which combination of scenarios is realised are complex, including the demand for types of youth labour, what incentives individual employers have to intervene in the school system in the general interest of capital; the outcome of GATS negotiations and the profitability of running schools; political parties' calculations of electoral considerations; and the extent of popular resistance, both at the political level and at the level of the subcultures of young people in the schools. Whether any of these scenarios would be more effective in producing the future workforce for capital is unclear. Predicting the future in education is an inexact science, as the many unexpected developments of the past decade illustrate, but the tentative conclusion of the analysis I have outlined is that employers will continue to make exactly the same complaints as they do today about the inability of the school system to produce the right sort of human capital. However, what can be predicted is that, whatever the extent of employer involvement, the continuation of the policies of diplomas and Academies will result in increased commodification of education, increased educational inequality and a further erosion of local democratic accountability in the school system.

There is one other possible scenario: the repossession of Academies from their private sponsors and their return to local democratic control; and the abandonment of academic-vocational segregation in favour of a common broad curriculum till age 16, as once proposed by HMI (DES, 1981, 1983) and more recently by the National Union of Teachers (NUT, 2005) and the Nuffield Review (Hayward *et al.*, 2006, ch. 5), incorporating a work-related element for all, designed to widen vocational horizons and develop critical understanding as well as foster certain skills. This would require a government which broke with the neo-liberal agenda for education, a scenario only conceivable as the result of mass popular opposition to the neo-liberal education agenda, of which current campaigns against Academies (Hatcher & Jones, 2006) perhaps provide an embryonic precursor.

References

Allen, M. (2007) Learning for Labour: specialist diplomas and 14–19 education, *Forum: for Promoting 3–19 Comprehensive Education*, 49(3), 299–304.

Allen, M. & Ainley, P. (2007) *Education make you fick, innit?* (London, Tufnell Press).

Anti-Academies Alliance (2008) *Attainment and progress in Academies—the facts* (London, Anti-Academies Alliance). Available online at www.antiacademies.org.uk (accessed 10 July 2008).

Avis, J. (2002) Work-based learning and social justice: 'learning to labour'? Paper presented at the *Annual Conference of the British Educational Research Association*, University of Exeter, 12–14 September. Available online at www.leeds.ac.uk/educol/documents/00002163.htm (accessed 10 July 2008).

Ball, S. J. (2007) *Education plc* (London, Routledge).

Ball, S. J. (2008) *The education debate* (Bristol, Policy Press).

Birmingham City Council (2006) *Building schools for the future: Birmingham's vision and strategy for secondary education* (Birmingham, BCC).

Blair, T. (2005) Speech at Sedgefield, 18 November.

Brown, G. (2007) Speech at Mansion House, 20 June.

Bulkley, K. E. (2007) Bringing the private into the public: changing the rules of the game and new regime politics in Philadelphia public education, *Educational Policy*, 21, 155–184.

CBI (Confederation of British Industry) (2008) *Taking stock: CBI education and skills survey 2008* (London, CBI).

City of Sunderland (2005) *Building schools for the future strategic business case* (Sunderland, City of Sunderland).

Conservative Party (2007) *Raising the bar, closing the gap* (London, The Conservative Party).

Cruddas, J. (2006) Neo-classical Labour, *Renewal*, 14(1), 34–41.

DES (Department of Education and Science) (1981) *Curriculum 11–16: a review of progress* (London, HMSO).

DES (Department of Education and Science) (1983) *Curriculum 11–16: towards a statement of entitlement* (London, HMSO).

DfES (Department of Education and Skills) (2005) *14–19 Education and Skills White Paper* (London, DfES).

Esland, G. (1996) Education, training and nation-state capitalism: Britain's failing strategy, in: J. Avis, M. Bloomer, G. Esland, D. Gleeson & P. Hodkinson (Eds) *Knowledge and nationhood: education, politics and work* (London, Cassell), 40–70.

Fullan, M. (2005) *Turnaround leadership* (San Francisco, Jossey-Bass).

Gibb, N. (2008) Statement quoted in ePolitix.com. 17 April. Available online at: www.epolitix.com/EN/ForumBriefs/200804/22c9ad16-cae3-4a8f-a672-4547d571b2e5.htm (accessed 30 April 2008).

Hatcher, R. (2006) Privatisation and sponsorship: the re-agenting of the school system in England, *Journal of Education Policy*, 21(5), 599–619.

Hatcher, R. & Jones, K. (2006) Researching resistance: campaigns against Academies in England, *British Journal of Educational Studies*, 54(3), 329–351.

Hayward, G., Hodgson, A., Johnson, J., Oancea, A., Pring, R., Spours, K., Wilde, S. & Wright, S. (2006) *The Nuffield Review of 14–19 education and training annual report 2005-06* (Oxford, University of Oxford Department of Educational Studies).

Higham, D. & Yeomans, J. (2006) *Emerging provision and practice in 14–19 education and training: a report on the evaluation of the third year of the 14–19 Pathfinder Initiative* (London, DES).

Hodgson, A., Keep, E. & Spours, K. (2007) *Nuffield Review issues paper 1: the new 14–19 diplomas* (Oxford, Nuffield Review).

Hodgson, A. & Spours, K. (2007) *Nuffield Review of 14–19 Education and Training issues paper 2: 14–19 partnerships: from weakly collaborative arrangements to strongly collaborative local learning systems* (Oxford, Nuffield Review).

Hopkins, D. (2007) *Every school a great school* (Maidenhead, Open University Press).

House of Commons Education and Skills Committee (2007) *14–19 diplomas: fifth report of session 2006–07* (London, The Stationery Office).

Jephcote, M. & Abbott, I. (2005) Tinkering and tailoring: the reform of 14–19 education in England, *Journal of Vocational Education and Training*, 57(2), 181–202.

Jones, K., Cunchillo, C., Hatcher, R., Hirtt, N., Innes, R., Johsua, S. & Klausenitzer, J. (2008) *Schooling in Western Europe: the new order and its adversaries* (Basingstoke, Palgrave Macmillan).

Keep, E. (2005) Reflections on the curious absence of employers, labour market incentives and labour market regulation in English 14–19 policy: first signs of a change in direction? *Journal of Education Policy*, 20(5), 533–553.

Leitch, S. (2006) *Prosperity for all in the global economy—world class skills* (London, HMSO).

Lipman, P. & Hursh, D. (2007) Renaissance 2010: the reassertion of ruling-class power through neoliberal policies in Chicago, *Policy Futures in Education*, 5(2), 160–178.

Manchester City Council (2006) *Transforming education and children's services: proposed academies programme & Wave 4 Bid for BSF* (Manchester, Manchester City Council).

Martin, R., Villeneuve-Smith, F., Marshall, L. & McKenzie, E. (2008) *Employability skills explored* (London, Learning and Skills Network).

Means, A. (2008) Neoliberalism and the politics of disposability: education, urbanization, and displacement in the new Chicago, *Journal for Critical Education Policy Studies*, 6(1). Available at: http://www.jceps.com/index.php?pageID=article&articleID=114 (accessed 10 July 2008).

National Union of Teachers (2005) *14–19 Bringing down the barriers* (London, NUT).

Nottingham City Council (2006) *Building schools for the future—strategic business case* (Nottingham, Nottingham City Council).

OECD (Organisation for Economic Cooperation and Development) (2002) *Rethinking human capital, education policy analysis* (Paris, OECD).

PricewaterhouseCoopers (2005) *Academies evaluation: 4th annual report* (London, PricewaterhouseCoopers).

PricewaterhouseCoopers (2007) *Academies evaluation: 4th annual report* (London, PricewaterhouseCoopers).

Tymms, P., Coe, R. & Merrell, C. (2005) *Standards in English schools: changes since 1997 and the impact of government policies and initiatives: a report for The Sunday Times* (Durham, CEM Centre, University of Durham).

Webster, P. & Frean, A. (2006) Prepare pupils for life, Blair tells teachers, *The Times*,30 November.

Whitfield, D. (2001) *Public services or corporate welfare* (London, Pluto Press).

Willetts, D. (2007) Better schools and more social mobility. Speech to the *CBI Conference on Public Service Reform*, 16 May.

14–19

Richard Pring

1. Seeing the young person 'as a whole'

There has for a long time been some ambivalence over whether wider social conditions should be held partly responsible for young people's achievements in schools. On the one hand, to admit to this would seem to let schools off the hook where the attainment of their students is less than the national expectations. Poverty should be no excuse for bad teaching. At present 636 schools have been judged to be struggling or failing; and their names have been made public (and in some cases surprised the governors and headteachers of the schools concerned). On the other hand, there is also a hesitant admission that poor results might partly be a function of the wider social and economic conditions. Recent research from the Institute of Education and the Institute of Fiscal Studies, commissioned for the Sutton Trust, shows that, out of the cohort of 600,000 11-year-olds starting secondary school in 1997, 60,000 in the top 20% (as measured in tests at 11, 14 and 16) failed to progress to university (Sutton Trust, 2008). In the vast majority of cases these came from households of considerable economic and social disadvantage. And certainly the quite considerable research from the Rowntree Foundation in the last ten years would point to the significance of poverty in the low attainment of many young people as they reach the end of their education, leaving school as soon as possible (or even before the compulsory leaving age) (Joseph Rowntree Foundation, 2007). The Youth Justice Board points to the increasing number of young people who are criminalised and indeed incarcerated.[1]

The recognition of the interrelationship of the different factors which affect educational performance, although not yet fully acknowledged in all aspects of policy, is reflected in the approach initiated by the Government to the general well-being of all young people up to the age of 19. Its White Paper *Every Child Matters,* published in 2003, set out the five aims for every young person, whatever the circumstances in which they lived:

Be healthy

Stay safe

Enjoy and achieve

Make a positive contribution

Achieve economic well-being.

The achievement of these aims requires a 'teaming up' of schools, health services, the police and voluntary bodies to protect young people from harm, and to help them live a more fruitful life—including educational success (DfES, 2003).

To implement this more holistic approach which, in theory at least, should affect profoundly the educational provision and understanding of young learners, there have been already major changes structurally. Local Education Authorities no longer exist, but have been subsumed under Local Authorities which have this wider and more integrated brief. This is reflected in the replacement of 'Chief Education Officers' by 'Directors of Children's Services'. In 2005, the first Children's Commissioner for England was appointed, with particular responsibility for the most vulnerable young persons.

The Children Act of 2004 translated these aspirations into legislation, establishing Children's Trusts in order to bring together all services for young people in a locality through 'inter-agency' co-operation. Indeed, the Act 'provided statutory guidance on inter-agency co-operation to improve the well-being of children'. This is important. Education is now officially seen as one aspect of 'well-being' (howsoever this is defined) and, reciprocally, 'well-being' is seen as a condition, generally speaking, for educational achievement. Hence, there is an attempt (supported by statute) to cut across erstwhile firm barriers between the professions.

Moreover, the guidance clearly stipulates that the 'voice of children, young people and their families should be heard at all levels in order to inform local design and delivery of the arrangements'.

What is declared to be a 'child-centred, outcome-led vision' would seem to be quite revolutionary—a major achievement *in conception* by the Labour administration. Of course, we need to wait and see, whether *in practice* it is a major achievement. There is a tension in any policy which aims to be both 'child-centred' and 'outcomes-led', for the 'leading outcomes' will be decided by officials, not by the children. Listening to the child's or young person's voice is all very well, but not if it is not allowed to shape the educational experience they have.

The integration of a range of social services around the perceived needs of the child would require a more central role for the Youth Service in education, and greater recognition in the provision of education of the many voluntary bodies which bring an expertise that often flourishes only outside the formal school structures. But the consequence of incorporating voluntary bodies within a statutory requirement carries its own risks. Perhaps the successful approaches of the more 'child centred' youth workers would not fit in with the 'outcomes-led vision' of *Every Child Matters.*[2]

The idea is welcome. But it would benefit from close research as it gets translated into practice. How are parenting groups enabled to contribute to the 'inter-agency' co-operation? Are the learning strategies, distinctive of the Youth Service support, being transferred into the more formal structures of the school? How far are the innovative practices of community policing (for example, in their pioneering introduction of 'restorative justice'[3]) to be maintained within the schools or colleges?

2. Personalisation of learning

'Personalised learning' is central to the fulfilment of the aims of *Every Child Matters*. In practical term it means 'focusing in a more structural way on each child's learning in order to enhance progress, achievement and participation' (DfES, 2003, p. 3). This is to be achieved through, amongst other things: learning connected to what the learners already know and experience (including outside the classroom); learners monitoring their learning and identifying the next steps; shifting the balance from class levels to individual progress; recognising and respecting the learner's voice; providing out of classroom support and advice; involvement of parents; recognition of non-cognitive factors and high order thinking skills; provision of different pathways and extension of choice; developing greater self-awareness. Indeed, the 'theory' of personalised learning would suggest that the learning needs of the young person should shape the learning programme rather than be shaped by targets and qualifications, and that there is a need to respond more effectively to the different, often more active, practical and experiential modes of learning of many young people.[4]

All this, however, seems an excellent example of the growing gap between rhetoric and reality, as the main determinant of the learning experience of young people is the regime of assessment hooked onto very specific learning targets, the attainment of which have become the 'performance indicators' for judging schools and their teachers.

3. Collaboration

Distinct from the requirements of the Children Act, although inevitably related, has been the policy thrust towards more collaborative arrangements between schools and colleges of further education. This was confirmed in the 2002 White Paper *Extending Opportunities, Raising Standards*. Indeed, it would be more appropriate now to talk about the development of a 'comprehensive federation' than 'comprehensive schools', as each school loses some of its autonomy in order to provide an 'entitlement' to the wide range of qualifications and opportunities in education and training post-14.

There are two causes of this development. The first has been the recognition that many young people in Key Stage 4 require a more practical and vocational learning experience than the school can offer. Therefore, arrangements have been made over several years for a substantial number of 14–16 year olds to attend Colleges of Further Education for part of the time. The 'Increased Flexibility Programme' (with over 100,000 14–16 year olds in any one year) demonstrated that the experience of practical, hands-on and occupationally-orientated learning is highly motivating (Higham & Yeomans, 2005).

The second cause is the development of the new Diplomas and, with them, the 'entitlement' of all 14–19 year olds by 2013 to be able to follow one of the 17 lines of Diploma, as well as the full range of GCSE and A-Level courses. Clearly that is not possible for any one school or college. Few, if any, schools have experts in 'hair and beauty', or the facilities for bricklaying or catering. Indeed, many schools with sixth forms may not be able to offer a full range of A Levels.

Indeed, the schools and colleges, in order to offer the Diploma, and thereby to access the money provided for it, need to go through a process which gives 'gateway status', thereby demonstrating that they are in a viable partnership.

There are several excellent examples, arising from this policy, of institutional collaboration (what the Nuffield Review has called 'strongly collaborative local learning systems') (Nuffield Review, 2007a). These might be characterised by common timetables, the appointment of a co-ordinator, transport between providers, recognition of different centres of expertise, strong links with training providers, local employers, possibly a local university, and a comprehensive and independent advisory system. In Kent and elsewhere, there have been developed 'Federations'—that is, the grouping of several schools under a single principal or head with a shared governing body.

This is a quite radical development of the institutional framework of education, but inevitably there are considerable difficulties in its attainment in many areas, especially where there is a tension in policy between promotion of partnership between schools, colleges, and higher education institutions and training providers, on the one hand, and practical encouragement of competition between them, on the other. Competition is exacerbated through different admissions arrangements, funding streams (e.g., unsustainable college subsidies for the 14–16 students in College of Further Education premises (Styles *et al.*, 2007)), post-16 developments (e.g., the creation of uneconomic sixth forms) and accountability based on the performance of individual (not partnerships of) institutions. Indeed, the differentiation of institutions rather than their collaboration has been a prominent part of government policy. Academies (independent but state-funded schools with their own admissions arrangements), City Technology Colleges (inherited from the Conservative administration), Specialist Schools, Faith Schools (both voluntary aided and voluntary controlled), Community Schools, Grammar Schools in some Local Authorities, sixth-form colleges and Colleges of Further Education—all provide a generally competing set of institutions, each with its own distinctive funding and admissions arrangements.

The Labour Government, therefore, has been quite radical in initiating 'collaborative learning systems' but (as the Nuffield Review, 2007a, points out) these remain weakly collaborative, not only because of the financial and organisational problems, but because they are handicapped by other policies.

The Local Authorities, deprived of so much of their power and influence in education, have been given a boost by the role assigned to them of establishing collaborative partnerships and of assigning the dedicated money. On the other hand, the exercise of these responsibilities is rendered difficult by the increased independence of the providers from their authority and control.

4. Qualifications reform

The reform of qualifications has been a priority of the Labour Government since 1997 (Nuffield Review, 2008a). But in this itself there is nothing new; qualifications at 16, 17 and 18 seem to have been in a constant state of flux. 1951 saw the introduction of the single subject General Certificate of Education, Ordinary (O) Level and Advanced (A) Level, to replace the School Certificate (which required a pass in a group of subjects). 1963 saw the introduction of the Certificate of Education (CSE) for those not deemed capable of taking O Levels. 1984 saw the introduction of the single examination at 16, GCSE, bringing together CSE and GCE O Level. Various attempts had been made to 'reform' A Level. Meanwhile, concern for those who did not pursue A Level post-16 was reflected in the constantly evolving (and short-lived) pre-vocational courses—CGL I 365 (City and Guilds of London Institute), CPVE (Certificate of Pre-vocational Education), and GNVQ (General National Vocational Qualification). Parallel with all these was a massive range of vocational qualifications run by such major examination bodies as the City and Guilds of London Institute, BTEC and Royal Society of the Arts (RSA), and by many professional bodies.

Therefore, it was felt strongly by the new Labour Government that greater simplicity was needed—a revision of some qualifications, a reduction of others, an 'equivalence' established between qualifications, and a clear progression through the qualifications into higher education, further training and employment. Qualification reform was high on the agenda.

A further reason for revision was the need for the national qualifications both to reflect and to encourage wider participation beyond the age of 16. What was referred to as 'the general route' (DCSF, 2008) would not be appropriate for many, although the majority would continue to follow that particular path.

An immediate problem was the narrowness of the post-16 choice of A Levels. To widen that choice, the A Level was split into two parts—the Advanced Subsidiary (AS) being taken after one year in a wider range of subjects (five was officially encouraged). However, the introduction of what was referred to as 'Curriculum 2000' was fraught with problems, particularly curriculum design. One significant consequence of this was the establishment of a committee under the former Chief Inspector of Schools, Mike Tomlinson. The Tomlinson Report (DCSF, 2004) proposed an overarching Diploma which could be taken at three different levels, and which would embrace different pathways—the more vocational and practical as well as the more academic. It would include an 'extended project' to enable the pursuit of a topic in depth as well as functional skills. The Report, therefore, was a major challenge to a system dominated by examinations which originated as a route for a minority into higher education, but had come to shape general education for the majority.

The Tomlinson Report was immediately rejected by the Secretary of State, Ruth Kelly, but, ironically, it remains as a major legacy of the Blair years. It was felt, politically, too great a challenge to the 'internationally-recognised standards' enshrined within the A Level. And yet, the Tomlinson Report had received, almost uniquely, widespread acceptance across the state and independent sectors of education, and among employer organisations. It had bravely tackled the academic/vocational divide; it had encouraged within a single framework a diversity of pathways; it had incorporated both relevance to the demands of the employers with its 'functional skills' and relevance to the demands of universities with its 'extended project'. As such, Tomlinson remains a reference point, a bench mark for future reforms.

The problems which Tomlinson tackled did not go away with its rejection. Therefore, a major development since 2004 has been the development parallel with the GCSE/A Level route, of 17 lines of Diploma, the first five of which were due to begin in September 2008. By 2013 all 17 will be taught, with an *entitlement* for all young people, wherever they are, to take any one of these Diplomas (Nuffield Review, 2007b).

That is what the present government would like to see as its legacy—a new, innovative set of pathways which would become the pathway of choice. Indeed, it has been referred to on many occasions as the most significant change in education since 1902—not therefore to be ignored in any account of the legacy of Blair's years in office.

Originally, these Diplomas were seen to be 'vocational'—developed by the Sector Skills Councils (representative of the many 'occupational sectors'), with the 'principal learning' related to an occupational interest, and with an element of practical work-based learning. In addition to this 'principal learning' will be 'generic learning' (including functional skills in English, mathematics and ICT, personal learning and thinking skills), and 'additional or specialist learning' (in which, for example, the young person would have the opportunity to study for an A Level). As such, they were conceived as a middle way between the 'academic' route, on the one hand, and 'vocational training' on the other. Their aim was broad—providing a more practical and vocational pathway into higher education, an occupationally relevant route into employment, and a more motivating learning experience for those disengaged from any further education and training.

The nomenclature has, however, constantly changed and they are no longer called 'vocational'. Indeed the final three new Diplomas, surprisingly announced in 2007, are in Science, Humanities and Languages.

The attempt to simplify the system of qualification into three major tracks (namely, academic, pre-vocational and vocational training) which, at three levels could be seen as somehow 'equivalent', was to be achieved in part by no longer funding students who might pursue alternative qualifications such as the BTEC national awards, and also by withdrawing the encouragement, previously given, for the International Baccalaureate to be an entitlement in every Local Authority.

However, the legacy of the Blair era would be seen to be an even more confusing array of qualifications, at different levels, than it had inherited. These might be summarised in the post-16 phase as:

- The general route GCSE/A Level, but with 'starred' A Grades to help highly selective universities to discriminate more effectively;
- 'Vocational' GCSE/A Levels, including 'applied' subjects such as Applied Science;
- International Baccalaureate, increasingly popular in the independent sector;
- A return by many universities to their own departmental entry tests;
- 17 lines of Diploma;
- BTEC Awards at different levels (which are gaining in popularity);
- OCR National Qualifications;
- National Vocational Qualifications (NVQs) at different levels;
- Levels 2 and 3 Apprenticeships with relevant technical certification.

5. Reforming work-based training and apprenticeships

Within the qualification framework, all qualifications are defined in terms of levels, and there is supposed to be some sort of equivalence between these levels—and also an attempt to define the levels of English qualifications in terms of those within a European Qualifications Framework. 'Equivalence' remains one of those undefined terms—and indeed might be an excellent example of where, in Wittgenstein's words (1958), there is an urgent need to move from 'disguised nonsense' to a recognition of what is 'patent nonsense'.

GCE 'A' Level qualifications are seen as Level 3; GCSE five A–Cs, Level 2. A successfully completed apprenticeship (which would include the technical know-how to do a skilled job) at Level 3 would be equivalent within the Qualification Framework to 'A' level. Similarly, successfully completed apprenticeships at Level 2 would be seen as equivalent to the five GCSE graded A to C.

The Government has set itself, in this regard, certain targets, namely:

- By 2015, 100% participation up to the age of 18 in education or training (bearing in mind that included in that 100% would be a large minority on work-based training);
- By 2013, 85% of all 19 year olds should have received a qualification at least at Level 2.[5]

This is, indeed, ambitious, although no more (in terms of participation) than was envisaged in the Fisher Act of 1918 and again in the 1944 Education Act.

The renewal of this aspiration, and the determination finally to make it a reality, has been a priority, reflected particularly, but not exclusively, in the reshaping of apprenticeships. Strong impetus was given by the findings (disputed though they now are) of the Leitch Review of Skills in 2006.[6] One response from the present Prime Minister reflects the importance attached to this:

> We plan a radical overhaul of apprenticeships … a new matching service … so that young people in any area can be matched up with businesses … a widening of the number of employers who now join the apprenticeship programme …[7]

The target for apprenticeships is 400,000 by 2020. The Government talked of an 'entitlement to an apprenticeship for every suitably qualified young person that wants one by 2013'. Indeed, the goal of 100% participation in some form of education and training would be made possible by the emphasis upon apprenticeships. In 2007, the Government announced a further increase in funding for apprenticeships in anticipation of an increase by 25%.

However, this requires a radical re-appraisal of apprenticeships for several reasons.

- For newer industries (for example, those connected with Information Technology) the traditional model of apprenticeships does not seem appropriate.
- There has been a major decline in those industries with which apprenticeships have been traditionally associated. For example, Rover Body and Pressings had 63 apprentices starting in 1960, but none in 2000.

This changing context was evident well before 1997. The Conservative government introduced 'Modern Apprenticeships' in 1994. But this did not stem the decline in work-based learning, which was at an all-time low in 2005, and particularly at Level 3 which would be regarded as the level at which young people would be deemed appropriately trained in certain but by no means all sectors (for example, in engineering, but not in hairdressing). Only 2.7% of the total 16–18 year old cohort reached Level 3 apprenticeship in 2005. It should be pointed out, however, that in this respect Britain is unlike Northern Europe and Scandinavia where Level 3 would be regarded as the norm for properly trained young workers in most sectors.

In many respects the Labour Government inherited a meaning of apprenticeship which had been changed by the previous administration, for traditional apprenticeship, unlike modern apprenticeships, involved a contract with an employer, under whom the key learning took place, with day release to the local college for theoretical support for the practical, work-based experience. The difficulties in renewing work-based learning, particularly the apprenticeship approach to this, are clearly set out by the Nuffield Review. The problems are deep-seated in the changing economic and social background. However, the problems do seem to be exacerbated by a lack of integrated 14–19 policy. In particular, the emphasis upon 50% of this age cohort proceeding to higher education and the introduction of Diplomas for many, who would not be prepared to study for A Levels, withdraws a large number from the pool of young people who would otherwise progress through the work-based apprenticeship route. Thereby, fewer at 18 are able to meet the need for the skills which the Leitch Report argues for.

The Labour Government has, in many ways, seen the problem. Its Cassels Committee reported on this in 2001 (DfES, 2001), and successfully argued for reforms. The failure to find enough employers has led to a strategy for programme-led (that is, college rather than work-based learning) apprenticeships in England. And the concept of 'apprentice' has changed—now including people in their twenties already in employment and undergoing in-house training, and also including many who have no contractual relationship with an employer.

But the problems are deep-seated, and it is to be seen whether the highly laudable government endeavours will meet the needs identified by Leitch.

6. Increased central management

Much of the Blair legacy has been but an extension of what was initiated by previous Conservative administrations. Continuity is more apparent than radical change. This is particularly reflected in the creation of Academies, which are but the offspring of the City Technology Colleges (independent but state-funded educational providers, sponsored by a range of individuals, businesses and religious foundations), and reflected too in the shifting of power and responsibility from local government (which once had local education authorities) to central government. It is reflected in the increased intervention in, and control over, the curriculum.

To grasp the significance of this change, one needs to recall the role of central government following the 1944 Education Act which emphasised the importance of a 'maintained system of education' which was locally controlled and which respected a degree of autonomy in the governance of voluntary aided and voluntary controlled schools. When Dr Marjorie Reeves was invited to join the Central Advisory Committee for Education (England) in 1947, she was told by the then Permanent Secretary, Redcliffe-Maud, that the main duty of the Committee was 'to be prepared to die at the first ditch as soon as politicians get their hands on education'.[8] When Prime Minister Callaghan became the first prime minister ever to give a major speech on education at Ruskin College in 1976, his political advisor was severely reprimanded by the Chief Inspector for Schools for writing a speech which had not been seen and indeed approved by her.[9]

The shift to central responsibility and direction was firmly embedded in the 1988 Education Reform Act which, amongst many other things, legislated for a national curriculum. What was to be learned in schools was to be determined very largely by the government's agencies.

This centralisation of responsibility for what is learned and for holding schools accountable to the public has been extended considerably in the 14–19 phase of education by the Labour Government, and that is reflected in the number of interventions affecting 14–19. The key White Paper was in 2005, namely *14–19 Education and Skills*. Following from this has been the rapid development of the Diplomas and the agreed 'gateway' to being allowed to teach them. The Leitch Review in 2006, 'Prosperity for all in the global economy: world class skills' set the tone for the 'skills revolution' which had been anticipated in the '21st Century Skills' White Paper, jointly from the DfES, DTI and DWP. This paper has already referred to the various interventions aimed at reforming the apprenticeship system and the system of qualification. However, preceding that 2005 'blueprint' for the future was a series of White Papers and Consultation Documents, advocating reform and pointing to the need for a 'skills revolution' if Britain was to succeed economically. *Learning to succeed: a new framework for post-16 learning* in 1999 set the tone with a single body (viz. the Learning and Skills Council) to oversee national strategy for post-16 learning. *Skills for life* in 2001 argued for a national strategy for improving adult literacy and numeracy skills; *Success for all* in 2001 described a programme for raising quality and effectiveness in colleges and training providers; *Schools achieving success* argued for more vocational routes and greater status for vocational awards. *Extending opportunities: raising standards*, also in 2002, emphasised local collaborative partnerships as a means of 'delivering' the wider educational and training opportunities. All these arguments were pulled together in *14–19 Opportunity and Excellence* in 2003. The Tomlinson review of qualifications, established in 2003, was, therefore, in part a response to all these papers—a reform of the qualifications system which would be comprehensive and which would find a respected place for more vocational and practical modes of learning.

Co-terminous with the increasing 'policy busyness' has been an intensifying of the language of management—a language of 'impacts', 'outcomes', 'performance indicators' and 'audits', of 'targets' and 'delivery'. Indeed, this changed language of education may be one of the major legacies of the Blair years, reflecting the belief that educational problems, which the government has 'identified', can be solved by central intervention and 'performance management' systems drawn from the world of commerce and business.[10]

7. Wales

The preceding pages refer predominantly, though not exclusively, to England. Since the devolving of responsibility for education and training in Wales by the Welsh Assembly Government (WAG) in 1997, Wales has, in certain important respects, pursued a different pathway (see particularly WAG, 2001, 2004). In *Learning country, learning pathways*, WAG set out its vision for the future for 14–19 young people, creating a wide range of motivating experiences and opportunities which go beyond the current statutory requirements, recognising the contribution which real life experiences and voluntary activities can make to the learning process, and emphasising flexibility in the kind of learning made possible, especially in terms of the pace of learning, supported by 'learning coaches'.

With regard to qualifications, Wales sees itself within a UK Qualifications Framework, but has created its own Welsh Baccalaureate which, although incorporating the traditional qualification of GCSE and A Level, seeks to provide a more coherent and comprehensive range of attainments from 14 to 19. It is an overarching award with a humanities component for all ('Wales, Europe and the World'), the Welsh language, community focused education and a greater emphasis on key skills (18% of the Baccalaureate). Although it is early days (about 50% of schools are now offering it), the Welsh Bac may be beginning to re-engage youngsters at all levels. It is designed for the 90th percentile.

Therefore, changes, reflecting 'clear red water' between policies in Wales and England (see Rees, 2003), took a broader view of education and training at 14–19. Reference was made to the creation, not only of a more 'vibrant economy' to be promoted, but also of a 'lively cultural and sporting life' and the advancement of 'the cause of social justice'.

Furthermore, Wales has maintained a thorough going community-based comprehensive school system—not creating the variety of competing kinds and differently funded schools as in England (no specialist schools or academies). The independent sector represents less than 1% of schools in Wales. It has abandoned national testing at 7, 11 and 14.

Conclusion

The legacy of the Blair years, therefore, with regard to 14–19 might be summarised as follows. First there is a marked shift of emphasis upon a 14–19 phase of education and training, in which there should be provision and entitlement for all young people, irrespective of background or ability.

Second, to achieve this there has been a determined (and, in many ways, laudable) effort to reform the qualifications framework and system of apprenticeships, to provide a more interagency and holistic approach to the well-being of all young people, and to require greater collaboration between different providers. These have been ambitious aims, changing the landscape of education, and the consequences of them cannot be fully appreciated for some time.

Third, however, the problems quite rightly identified (for example, the academic/vocational divide, the low status attached to vocational, the decline of apprenticeships and work-based learning) are deep rooted, economically and socially. And the solutions pursued with such vigour (for example, the proposed reform of qualifications and of apprenticeships) could well be but a continuation of a long line of 'reforms' which do not work. In that respect, the most important legacy might be greater understanding of the problems, and a more humble approach to their long term solutions.

Notes

1. See Youth Justice Board Annual Statistics, February 2006, and Morgan & Newburn (2007).
2. See Nuffield Review Issues Paper 11, 2008, *Lessons from detached youth work,* which points to the difficulty of maintaining its distinctive pedagogy once the Youth Service is incorporated within the school system.
3. See Youth Justice Board, 2005, *Restorative Justice in Schools*, for a well researched account of the benefits of this aspect of the wider community involvement with schools.
4. See Hargreaves, 2007, for an expansion on these points about 'personalised learning'.
5. See Nuffield Review, 2008b, c.
6. see Leitch, 2006; Keep, 2007.
7. Quoted in Nuffield Review Issues Paper 3. The reports and research referred to in the following paragraphs are to be found in that Issues Paper.

8. In conversation with Richard Pring before her death in 2004.
9. Talk given by Lord Donoghue, formerly adviser to Prime Minister Callaghan, at University of Oxford Department of Educational Studies, 2002.
10. See Nuffield Review, 2008, Issues Paper No. 7, *Aims and values,* for a critique of this change of language.

References

DCSF (Department for Children, Schools and Families) (2004) *14–19 Curriculum and qualification reform: final report of the working group* (Tomlinson Report) (London, DCSF).

DCSF (Department for Children, Schools and Families) (2006) *Prosperity for all in the global economy: world class skills* (Leitch Review of Skills) (London, DCSF).

DCSF (Department for Children, Schools and Families) (2008) *Promoting achievement, valuing success: a strategy for the 14–19 qualifications* (London, DCSF).

DfES (Department for Education and Skills) (2001) *Modern apprenticeships: the way to work* (Cassells Report) (London, DfES).

DfES (Department for Education and Skills) (2003) *Every child matters* (London, DfES).

Hargreaves, D. (2007) Paper to the Specialist Schools and Academies Trust, reported in *The Times Educational Supplement,* 16 November.

Higham, J. & Yeomans, D. (2005) *Collaborative approaches to 14–19 provision.* Report of the Second Year of the 14–19 Pathfinder Initiative, University of Nottingham.

Joseph Rowntree Foundation (2007) *Experiences of poverty and educational disadvantage* (York, Joseph Rowntree Foundation).

Keep, E. (2007) Leitch and after, *Adult Learning,* NIACE Journal, September.

Morgan, G. & Newburn, T. (2007) Juvenile justice, in: M. McGuire *et al.* (Eds) *Oxford handbook of criminology* (4th edn.) (Oxford, Oxford University Press).

Nuffield Review (2007a) *Issues Paper no 2: 14–19 partnerships: from weakly collaborative arrangement to strongly collaborative local learning systems.* Available at: www.nuffield14-19review.org.uk.

Nuffield Review (2007b) *Issues Paper no 1: The new 14–19 diplomas.* Available at: www.nuffield14-19review.org.uk.

Nuffield Review (2008a) *Issues Paper no 10: General education in the 14–19 phase.* Available at: www.nuffield14-19review.org.uk

Nuffield Review (2008b) *Issues Paper no. 3: Apprenticeships: prospects for growth.* Available at: www.nuffield14-19review.org.

Nuffield Review (2008c) *Issues Paper no. 4: Apprenticeships II: a high quality pathway for young people*

Rees, G. (2003) *Democratic devolution and education policy in Wales: the emergence of a national system?* (Cardiff, Cardiff University School of Social Science).

Styles, P., Fletcher, M. & Valentine, R. (2007) *Implementing 14–19 provision: a focus on schools* (London, LSC Research Report).

Sutton Trust (2008) *Wasted Talent? Attention rates for high-achieving pupils between school and university* (London, Institute of Education and the Institute for Fiscal Studies).

Welsh Assembly Government (WAG) (2001) *Learning country, learning pathways* (Cardiff, WAG).

Welsh Assembly Government (WAG) (2004) *Learning country, learning pathways: implementation plan* (Cardiff, WAG).

Wittgenstein, L. (1958) *Philosophical investigations* (Oxford, Blackwell).

Faith-based schools in England after ten years of Tony Blair

Geoffrey Walford

Introduction

It is common for commentators to claim that many of Blair's educational policies were largely a continuation of those of the previous Conservative governments. It is certainly correct that Margaret Thatcher's push towards marketisation and privatisation of schooling, along with a greater emphasis on 'choice and diversity', was continued and amplified during Blair's time in office. But, while these continuities are important to understanding the Blair legacy, so are the discontinuities—and these are partly linked to Blair's personal Christian faith and to the role that he believed faith should have in society (Blair, 2008). Blair's policies to increase the number of faith schools and to open the opportunity for state-funding to schools for a wider range of minority faiths has been highly controversial for three main reasons. First, it is argued that segregation of minority faith students (and thus often students of minority ethnicities) into separate schools is highly undesirable and could lead to greater ethnic tensions in the future. Second, it is claimed that many Roman Catholic schools and some Church of England schools indirectly select students according to social class, and that the Christian ethos and demands of these schools act to exclude students from some ethnic minorities. Third, the curriculum of some faith schools may inculcate intolerant and bigoted views. In this article I will trace some of the continuities and discontinuities in policy with regard to faith schools and make an evaluation of Blair's legacy in this area.

Faith schools before Blair

Historically, faith schools have been at the centre of the English education system. It was only following the 1870 *Education Act* that the state became involved in the provision, maintenance and organisation of its own elementary schools. A national system was established, but one where responsibility for provision was still shared with several different faith-based providers. The 1902 and 1944 *Education Acts* for England and Wales built upon this existing understanding. The schools provided by the religious groups constituted the vast majority of the so-called voluntary schools where buildings were owned by the religious group but current expenditure was given by the state. This sector was divided into two parts with most Catholic schools becoming voluntary aided and most Church of England schools being voluntary controlled, the major differences being that voluntary aided schools had a majority of church-appointed school governors on their Boards, and paid a larger part of any new building costs.

In 1979, when Margaret Thatcher came to power, about 28% of primary aged pupils in maintained schools were in voluntary schools, as were 17% of secondary pupils. Over all ages, 22% of pupils were in this voluntary sector, of which 11% were Church of England, 9% Roman Catholic, and less than 1% each of Jewish and Methodist (O'Keeffe, 1986). A further 7% of school-age children were in private schools, most of which were originally established by church-related groups or individuals.

The years after 1960 were marked by both the growth of secularism and considerable increases in the numbers of children from ethnic and religious minorities. For example, by the mid-1990s there were about a million Muslims in England, with about 75% having origins in the Indian subcontinent (Vertovec, 2002), and about 400,000 children of Muslim parents of school age in England (Sarwar, 1994). Most of these were in schools provided by the local education authorities. But some parents valued a religious ethos, so a considerable number of Muslim, Sikh and Hindu children were in Church of England schools (where some urban schools even had Muslim majorities), some were in Roman Catholic schools and a few in Jewish schools. While not being a stated government policy, during most of the post-war period, growing secularism and multiculturalism had led to a de-emphasis on Christian religious teaching and to a large scale abandonment of the theoretically compulsory daily act of worship in all schools. Within areas of high ethnic minority concentration—such as parts of London, Bradford and Birmingham—the Anglican schools, in particular, had often accommodated many of the religious needs of all children and, while a Christian ethos remained, there was positive acceptance of other faiths.

From sponsored grant-maintained schools to diversity of faith-based schools

One of the groups who perceived a growing secularism within most state-maintained schools—including those voluntary schools run by the churches—were evangelical Christians, who established their own small private schools where they could ensure that their own Christian beliefs were fully reflected in the teaching and ethos (Walford, 2000a). Similarly, this perception of growing secularism, alongside a growing confidence within ethnic minority communities, also led to concern amongst various other religious minority parents—in particular Muslim parents who believed that their children were likely to be drawn away from their Islamic belief and practices. As a result, in the late 1980s, various groups established small private Muslim schools for their children.

The Conservative government's *Education Reform Act* of 1988 made it possible for schools to 'opt-out' of Local Education Authority control to become grant-maintained schools which received funding from central rather than local government. A shaky coalition of groups (representing Muslims, Evangelical Christians, small schools and others) worked together to establish the possibility that existing private schools or new schools could 'opt-in' and become a new type of grant-maintained school which included a sponsor (Walford, 2000b; Parker-Jenkins, 2002). From April 1994, it became possible for groups of parents, and charitable, religious or independent sponsors or promoters to apply to establish their own grant-maintained schools. Groups of sponsors could propose either the establishment of an entirely new school or that an existing faith-based or other private school should be re-established as a grant-maintained school. Final decisions were made by the Secretary of State.

The process of application and approval was slow so that, by the time of the General Election in May 1997, in England only 20 full proposals had been published. The Conservative government had agreed to just seven of these—six being the transfer of existing private Roman Catholic secondary schools and one being an existing Jewish primary school. The Conservative government was operating the scheme in a way similar to a franchise (Walford, 1997) with no real increase in the diversity of schooling on offer.

When Labour came to power in 1997 it quickly introduced a White Paper, *Excellence in Schools* (DfEE, 1997), which proposed a new organisational structure for schools and the abolition of grant-maintained status. It also made it clear that no new proposals for sponsored grant-maintained schools would be considered, but that voluntary status would be possible. It finally accepted seven of the ten existing applications as voluntary-aided schools, including two further Roman Catholic schools, one further Jewish school and, much more significantly, two Muslim primary schools and one Seventh Day Adventist secondary school. It was thus Blair's government that made the decision to fund a greater range of schools for religious minorities. The Conservatives had brought forward the legislation but, in the period before a General Election, they had not made any potentially controversial decisions.

By January 2007, there were 37 Jewish schools, two Sikh, seven Muslim, one Seventh Day Adventist and one Greek Orthodox, along with 26 Methodist, 4642 Church of England, 2038 Roman Catholic, and 86 other Christian schools. The first Hindu school opened in September 2008. As there were 20,704 maintained schools, this means that 33% of maintained schools were faith-based. Surprisingly, the percentage of children in faith-based maintained schools and the percentage of faith-based schools have remained practically static. In 1998, 33% of maintained schools were faith-based, and 24.8% of pupils in maintained schools were in faith-based schools. In 2007 this had fallen slightly to 23.4% of pupils. However, these figures do not tell the whole story.

From City Technology Colleges to City Academies

A second idea from the Conservatives that Labour has developed is that of City Technology Colleges, which were to be jointly funded by central government and industrial sponsors. As the name suggests, City Technology Colleges were to provide a curriculum rich in science and technology, but they were also designed for a specific group of 11 to 18 year olds from the 'inner city'. One major feature was that they were to be private or independent schools, run by charitable trusts, with the sponsors having a major influence on the way in which the Colleges were managed. These sponsors were also intended to provide substantial financial and material support (DES, 1986; Walford & Miller, 1991; Whitty *et al.*, 1993). It is of note that the only mention of faith in the original document is a clear statement that 'Admission to CTCs will not be subject to any denominational test' (DES, 1986, p. 5).

The reaction to the announcement of CTCs was frosty. Very few industrialists showed their 'wish to help extend the range of choice for families in urban areas', and many were openly hostile to the idea. All of the early sponsors were strong supporters of the Conservative Party, but even they were unprepared to donate anything like the proportion of the funds that had been originally envisaged. The CTCs proved much more expensive to establish than was first thought, and sponsors provided only about 20% of the capital expenditure and little of the current expenditure (Walford & Miller, 1991).

As major industrial and technological companies were reluctant to be involved, smaller and less glamorous sponsors had to be persuaded to take part. In this atmosphere, sponsors with religious links became involved. For example, the Southwark Diocesan Board of Education of the Church of England had a school in urgent need of new accommodation. The DES had twice refused to approve the necessary capital expenditure, but welcomed the idea that it should become a new CTC in London Docklands (Whitty *et al.*, 1993, p. 47). In Gateshead, a group of evangelical Christians approached Peter Vardy, a local Christian entrepreneur who ran a chain of car dealerships, to sponsor a new CTC. The resulting Emmanuel CTC has been the site of continual controversy for issues such as high rates of exclusion, the teaching of creationism, homophobia and its discipline policies. While not selecting students or parents on faith, Emmanuel CTC puts forward a Biblically-based evangelical Christianity.

The CTC programme came to a halt in 1991 with just 15 CTCs and only about 20% of capital funding having been provided by sponsors. Two of these were explicitly faith-based, but both came into existence more to try to support a flagging policy than from any real desire from government to increase faith-based schooling. Kenneth Baker's (1993, p. 185) account of the City Technology Colleges does not mention faith at all except to note that the Catholic Church was against the policy, but was pragmatic enough to sell redundant school buildings and sites to become CTCs.

Given the difficulties that the Conservative government had experienced in trying to obtain sponsorship for CTCs, it is strange that Blair's Labour government should eventually resurrect the policy in the form of City Academies. In 2000 David Blunkett, then Secretary of State, announced that 'City Academies' were to be created—officially independent schools, but maintained by the state. They were to have sponsors who would give £2 million towards the capital costs and who would henceforth have a controlling interest in the school. This time they were not restricted to technology, but could also specialise in modern foreign languages, visual arts, performing arts or media arts, sport or 'any subject specified by order of the Secretary of State'. Their close similarity with the CTCs was emphasised by the fact that the legislation in the *Learning and Skills Act* 2000 simply amended the CTC legislation as it was in the *Education Act* 1996. Various difficulties with the policy led to further changes in the *Education Act* 2002 including the word 'City' being dropped such that these new schools became simply 'Academies'. Schedule 7 to that Act also made special provisions for Academies where the premises was originally linked to the Church of England or where a member of the governing body of an Academy is appointed to represent the interests of the Church of England. Such Academies became officially 'church schools'.

In many ways the story of the Academies echoes that of the CTCs, but Blair's government was far more generous in its financial support and other assistance. Sponsors have been able to donate 'in kind' to an extraordinary extent, and the average cost of the first 12 Academies was £23 million (Beckett, 2007, p. 13). Faith groups have seen this as an economical way of building their own schools, and the Blair government was active in trying to attract faith groups to become sponsors.

In February 2008 there were 83 Academies in operation, with several more due to open in future years (DCSF, 2008) and a plan for 400 by 2010. Five of this total are re-named City Technology Colleges, and it is likely that more will make the change. Of these 83, 27 can be defined as having a religious character. These 27 are listed in Table 1. At 33%, this number gives a similar percentage of faith schools to national figures for all schools. There is considerable diversity among these schools. First, nine of these are clearly Church of England, two clearly Roman Catholic, but there are 16 which are designated Christian, including one sponsored jointly by the Church of England and the Roman Catholic Church. Two of the Academies—The King's Academy and Trinity Academy—are sponsored by the Emmanuel Schools Foundation which is the sponsoring body for Sir Peter Vardy's Emmanuel School (Green, 2008). The Foundation has said that it would be prepared to sponsor another ten academies within the North of England. Critics have been particularly concerned about these two Academies because of their strong evangelical Christian sponsorship, the teaching of creationism, high exclusion rates and homophobia (Beckett, 2007, pp. 68–85; Gillard, 2007, p. 218). Another nine of these Academies are sponsored by the United Learning Trust, which is a Christian educational charity created specifically to sponsor academies and a subsidiary of the United

Church Schools Trust, which was formerly the Church Schools Company founded in 1883 and currently controlling ten private schools in England.

It is worth noting that none of the 83 Academies is sponsored by a non-Christian faith group.

Supporting faith schools

Blair's support for faith schools was evident from very early in his Premiership. He believed that faith schools have a particular 'ethos' that is distinct and that encourages moral development as well as academic success. The General Synod of the Church of England declared in 1998 that 'church schools stand at the centre of the Church's mission to the nation' (Chadwick, 2001) and, in 2000, the Archbishops' Council of

Table 1. Academies having a defined religious character as at February 2008 (DCSF, 2008)

Academy	Sponsoring body
Bradford Academy	Diocese of Bradford
Burlington Danes Academy	Absolute Return for Kids ARK
David Young Community Academy	Diocese of Ripon and Leeds
Eastbourne Church of England Academy	Church of England
Folkestone Academy	Roger de Haan & Kings School Canterbury
Greig City Academy	The Greig Trust with the Diocese of London
Lambeth Academy	United Learning Trust
Manchester Academy	United Learning Trust and Manchester Science Trust
Northampton Academy	United Learning Trust
Oasis Academy Enfield	Oasis Trust
Paddington Academy	United Learning Trust
Salford City Academy	United Learning Trust
Sheffield Park Academy	United Learning Trust
Sheffield Springs Academy	United Learning Trust
St Anne's Academy	Church of England & David and Anne Crossland
St Matthew Academy	Roman Catholic
St Mark's Church of England Academy	Southwark Diocese, Toc H and CfBT Education Trust
St Mary Magdalene Academy	Church of England
St Michael and All Angels C of E Academy	Church of England
St Paul's Academy	Roman Catholic Diocese of Southwark
Stockport Academy	United Learning Trust
The Academy of St Francis of Assisi	Diocese of Liverpool and The Roman Catholic Archdiocese of Liverpool
The Barnsley Academy	United Learning Trust
The King's Academy	Emmanuel Schools Foundation
The Samworth Enterprise Academy	Church of England
Trinity Academy	Emmanuel Schools Foundation
Walthamstow Academy	United Learning Trust

the Church of England established a Church Schools Review Group with Lord Dearing as Chair (Dearing Report, 2001). Its recommendations included an expansion in the number of Anglican secondary schools (which were seen as inclusive, and catering for students of all faiths and none), which Tony Blair quickly supported. One hundred new schools were proposed, and the Church of England has made considerable progress towards that target through Academies as well as though voluntary status. By mid-2008 (Church of England, 2008) there were 12 Academies linked to the Church of England (excluding those linked to the United Learning Trust)—four of which were based on existing Church of England schools—and 31 new voluntary schools. There were also a further 18 Academies agreed for the future—nine based on existing Church of England schools—and five new voluntary schools. As at June 2007 there were a further 82 projects (including 53 Academies) under discussion but many of these were not expected to come to fruition. Many of these sponsorships are in collaboration with other partners. In spite of these new schools, the overall number of Church of England schools is in decline, but this is mainly due to closure of small primary schools in line with population demographics. In 1997 there were 4775 Church of England schools, but only 4651 (including nine Academies) in 2007. In the same period Catholic schools had decreased from 2132 to 2038 and Methodist schools from 28 to 26. In contrast, Jewish schools had increased from 24 to 37.

In June 2001 the government announced that it was cutting the capital contribution for voluntary-aided schools from 15% to 10%, thus reducing the amount that faith groups would have to pay to establish new schools. In the White Paper *Schools Achieving Success* (DfES, 2001, p. 45) support was given to 'inclusive faith schools', and it was stated that School Organisation Committees would be required to give proposals for new schools from faith groups the same consideration as those from the local authority. Officially, where there was local support, the government welcomed new schools from the Church of England, non-denominational groups and those of other faiths in order to 'add to the inclusiveness and diversity of the system'. Some 45 Labour MPs defied the party whip and tried to make all new faith schools accept at least 25% of students from other faiths or none. This was defeated.

During Blair's third term of office his support for faith schools increased. Recognising that there were still few Muslim, Hindu or Sikh schools in the state sector, the White Paper, *Higher Standards, Better Schools for All* (DfES, 2005) proposed that it should be easier for independent schools to enter the new system and that all schools should be able to become Trust schools somewhat similar to Academies. The White Paper specifically mentions that the government had already funded consultancy support to the Association of Muslim Schools to help schools make the transition (£100,000) (DfES, 2005, p. 31).

Again, one driving force behind this was the desire to enable every school 'to be free to develop a distinctive ethos and to shape its curriculum, organisation and use of resources' (DfES, 2005, p. 25). Equally importantly, the White Paper stated that 'We will encourage voluntary controlled schools—most of which are Church of England primary schools—to become Trust schools. This will, for the first time, enable their existing Trusts to appoint the majority of the governing body—an advantage currently enjoyed by voluntary aided schools' (DfES, 2005, p. 27). While giving more control to the Churches may be an advantage for them, it is less clear that it is a universal advantage even if, as envisaged, 'Trusts will also be under a duty to promote community cohesion and good race relations' (DfES, 2005, p. 29). In contrast, at about the same time, an opinion poll for *the Guardian* found that 64% of their respondents believed that the government should not be funding religious schools of any kind (ICM, 2005).

Keeping the faith

The Blair government's encouragement of faith-based schools was officially linked to a belief that faith schools have a particular ethos that supports the development of morality and of high academic achievement. This belief was supplemented by the additional one—that faith schools could be inclusive and teach social cohesion. It is difficult to test this type of faith against evidence but, where it is possible, the evidence is at best mixed.

It is certainly true that, on average, students at faith schools obtain better educational qualifications than those at non-faith schools, but it is widely argued that this is due to selection of more able higher social class students and parents. A survey by the Institute for Research in Integrated Strategies (IRIS) of 17,000 children in Church of England and Catholic primary schools in 2006 showed that that there is a social class bias in their intakes, with 13.96% of children being eligible for free school meals as opposed to 19.96% in the catchment areas (Gillard, 2007, p. 222). West (forthcoming) examined the situation for religious schools in London by using data from the National Pupil Database for 2005. She found that, while there were considerable differences between individual schools, overall, just 17% of children in religious schools were eligible for free school meals compared with 25% in non-religious schools. They also educated a smaller proportion of the lowest ability pupils (19% versus 31%). Pupils from all South Asian minority ethnic groups were under-represented, with just 1% of Pakistani and Bangladeshi students in religious schools, while Black African and Caribbean ethnic groups were over-represented. However, within this group of Black ethnicity students, those who attended religious schools were less likely to be eligible for free school meals (24% versus 37%) (see also Chamberlain *et al.*, 2006; West & Hind, 2007).

With such intakes, it is to be expected that faith-based schools would achieve higher educational results. But, surprisingly, in value added terms, their success is much less clear. Schagen and Schagen (2005) examined national value-added datasets to evaluate the school effects at primary and secondary levels. They found that Jewish schools did perform better than other schools in value added terms, but that on balance Roman Catholic schools did not perform any better or worse than other schools. Church of England schools had some significant positive achievements, but the differences were slight.

Of course, many religious parents choose faith schools simply because they wish their children to attend schools where faith is valued and encouraged but, sadly, there are sometimes rather less positive reasons. Dench *et al.* (2006) show how life has changed in the East End of London since the famous account given in *Family and Kinship in East London* (Young & Willmott, 1957). The authors argue that many white working-class families have taken refuge in local Christian schools rather than use the non-denominational community schools. According to the 2001 census, in the London Borough of Tower Hamlets 58% of those aged 0–17 were of Bangladeshi origins yet, in 2002, 17 primary schools had over 90% Bangladeshi children, while nine (all denominational) had fewer than 10%. Out of 16 secondary schools, four denominational schools each had 3% or fewer Bangladeshi children while three nearby non-denominational schools had over 80%. This represents severe ethnic segregation of the local population.

The Blair legacy?

It is clear that considerable encouragement was given to faith schools during Tony Blair's Premiership. It was Blair who gave state support to schools for a wider range of religious minorities, and encouraged the expansion of faith schools both in the voluntary and Academies sector. Further encouragement for faith schools was given by the joint declaration *Faith in the education system* (DCSF, 2007) of September 2007. In practice, only a small number of Muslim, Sikh and Greek Orthodox schools have entered the maintained system, the number of Church of England and Roman Catholic schools has declined, and Jewish schools have increased. However, the Church of England has been active in proposing new Academies and voluntary schools, and many of these are secondary schools.

The main legacy is no doubt a slightly more diverse and more multi-faith system of schools in the state-maintained sector. But it is difficult to see how any other government could have not agreed to funding Muslim, Sikh, Hindu and other minority faith schools, given that various types of Christian and Jewish schools had this advantage. The growing confidence of these groups to take an active part in the democratic government of Britain, and to take advantage of what it has to offer, led to pressures which it would have been difficult for any government to counteract. Only by removing or reducing funding from Christian and Jewish faith schools would it have been possible for such requests to have been denied.

The odd aspect of encouraging more faith schools is that far from all religious groups actually want separate schools for their children. Most would be satisfied if the particular requirements of their faith were respected within common schools. While it is possible that separate schooling need not lead to a fragmentation of society and increased racism (Short, 2003), there is less chance of this happening if schools have a mix of children from different social classes, ethnicities and religions. The desire for cultural continuity can be achieved without the need for separation (Walford, 2008).

Blair's support for faith schools probably may have fewer long-term effects than he expected. Changes to legislation since Blair left office have made it a requirement that Local Authorities are involved in decisions about Academies. This has meant, for example, that a proposal from the Emmanuel School Foundation for further

Evangelical Christian Academies in Durham was rejected by Durham County Council. This was in spite of personal support from Tony Blair (Wood, 2008). The Christian churches have only partially exploited the possibilities offered to them and, indeed, many within the churches question the desirability of any expansion. Similarly, the number of minority faith voluntary schools is still small. In all, Blair may have simply delayed the inevitable debate that is needed about the role of faith-based schools in a modern society (Judge, 2001).

Acknowledgements

I thank Beth Green, John Gay and two independent referees for their insightful comments on an earlier version of this article.

References

Baker, K. (1993) *The turbulent years. My life in politics* (London, Faber & Faber).

Beckett, F. (2007) *The great City Academy fraud* (London, Continuum).

Blair, T. (2008) Faith and globalisation. Speech given at the Cardinal Lectures, Westminster Cathedral, London, 3 April. Available online at: http://tonyblairoffice/speeches/.

Chadwick, P. (2001) The Anglican perspective on Church schools, *Oxford Review of Education,* 27(4), 475–487.

Chamberlain, T., Rutt, S. & Fletcher-Campbell, F. (2006) *Admissions: Who goes where? Messages from the statistics. LGA Research Report 4/06* (Slough, NFER).

Church of England (2008) Private communication.

Dearing Report (2001) *The way ahead: Church of England schools in the new millennium,* Report of the Church Schools Review Group (London, Church House Publishing).

Dench, G., Gavron, K. & Young, M. (2006) *The new East End: kinship, race and conflict* (London, Profile Books).

DCSF (Department for Children, Schools and Families) (2007) *Faith in the education system* (London, DCSF).

DCSF (Department for Children, Schools and Families) (2008) Available at: http://wwwedu-base.gov.uk/EstablishmentFindDownload.aspx?type=CSV (accessed 14 February 2008).

DfEE (Department for Education and Employment) (1997) *Excellence in schools* (London, The Stationery Office).

DES (Department of Education and Science) (1986) *City Technology Colleges. A new type of school* (London, DES).

DfES (Department for Education and Skills) (2001) *Schools achieving success* (London, The Stationery Office).

DfES (Department for Education and Skills) (2005) *Higher standards, better schools for all* (London, The Stationery Office).

Gillard, D. (2007) Never mind the evidence: Blair's obsession with faith schools, *Forum,* 49(3), 213–228.

Green, E. (2008) Exploring the relationship between core values, school discipline and student culture at a City Technology College with a Bible-based Christian ethos. Paper given at the *St Hilda's Ethnography and Education Conference,* Oxford, September.

ICM (2005) Guardian Opinion Poll, Fieldwork 12–14 August.

Judge, H. (2001) Faith-based schools and state funding: a partial argument, *Oxford Review of Education,* 27(4), 463–474.

O'Keeffe, B. (1986) *Faith, culture and the dual system* (London, Falmer).

Parker-Jenkins, M. (2002) Equal access to state funding: the case of Muslim schools in Britain, *Race Ethnicity and Education,* 5(3), 273–289.

Sarwar, G. (1994) *British Muslims and schools* (London, Muslim Education Trust).

Schagen, I. & Schagen, S. (2005) The impact of faith schools on pupil performance, in: R. Gardner, J. Cairns & D. Lawton (Eds) *Faith schools. Consensus or conflict?* (London, RoutledgeFalmer).

Short, G. (2003) Faith schools and social cohesion: opening up the debate, *British Journal of Religious Education,* 25(2), 129–141.

Vertovec, S. (2002). Islamophobia and Muslim recognition in Britain, in: Y. Haddad (Ed.) *Muslims in the West: from sojourners to citizens* (Oxford, Oxford University Press).

Walford, G. (1997) Sponsored grant-maintained schools: extending the franchise? *Oxford Review of Education,* 23(1), 31–44.

Walford, G. (2000a) *Policy and politics in education. Sponsored grant-maintained schools and religious diversity* (Aldershot, Ashgate).

Walford, G. (2000b) From City Technology Colleges to sponsored grant-maintained schools, *Oxford Review of Education,* 26(2), 145–158.

Walford, G. (2008) Muslim schools in England and the Netherlands: sustaining cultural continuity, in: Z. Bekerman & E. Kopelowitz (Eds) *Cultural education—cultural sustainability: minority, diaspora, indigenous and ethno-religious groups in multicultural societies* (London, Lawrence Erlbaum Associates), 13–30.

Walford, G. & Miller, H. (1991) *City Technology College* (Buckingham, Open University Press).

West, A. (forthcoming) Religious schools in London: school admissions, religious composition and selectivity, *Oxford Review of Education.*

West, A. & Hind, A. (2007) School choice in London, England: Characteristics of students in different types of secondary school, *Peabody Journal of Education,* 82(2–3), 498–529.

Whitty, G., Edwards, T. & Gewirtz, S. (1993) *Specialisation and choice in urban education. The City Technology College experiment* (London, Routledge).

Wood, S. (2008) Still no-go on academy, *The Journal,* 13 March.

Young, M. & Willmott, P. (1957) *Family and kinship in East London* (London, Routledge & Kegan Paul).

Realising the potential of new technology? Assessing the legacy of New Labour's ICT agenda 1997–2007

Neil Selwyn

Introduction

In seeking to assess the legacy of Tony Blair's emphasis on education as a 'driving mission' during his time in office (Brown, 2007) one would be forgiven for concentrating solely on the high-profile changes in areas such as school governance, curriculum and qualifications reform, national literacy and numeracy strategies, and the expansion of higher education. Yet as the theme of this special issue of the *Oxford Review of Education* implies, the Blair administration leaves a legacy of systemic educational change above and beyond its 'headline' policies of education re-organisation and re-provision. In particular this paper focuses on Blair's legacy in terms of the specific aim of 'realising the potential of new technology'—a central educational theme within the 1997 Labour election manifesto. In practical terms the ten years following Blair's election to Prime Minister saw the positioning of 'information and communications technology' (ICT) as a major presence in the UK education system. Moreover, New Labour's (re)discovery of education technology as a distinct policy area allowed the party to make great play of branding itself the 'pioneer of new thinking' in relations to its political rivals. Now eleven years after the party's initial proposals for 'connecting the learning society' it is possible to offer a detached critical analysis of New Labour's ICT drive during the 1997 to 2007 period and consider the legacy of these policies in terms of the ongoing technological enhancement of the UK education system.

From the outset of such an analysis one must, of course, be mindful of maintaining a sense of perspective on the relative significance of New Labour's education ICT policies. Indeed, when compared to what are now being touted as the major achievements of the Blair administration the area of educational ICT would seem to merit only a minor footnote—not least when set against New Labour's establishment of economic competence; heightened investment in public services; introduction of redistributive mechanisms such as the minimum wage and *Sure-Start*; and devolution of governance to the home nations (Giddens, 2007). Moreover, education was just one of many segments of the public sector which were subject to so-called 'information age' policymaking between 1997 and 2007—with technology-based interventions applied to areas such as the delivery of central and local 'e-government' services, to the administration of health, welfare, social security, criminal justice, policing and other public sector services (see Selwyn, 2002a; Hudson, 2002; Peckover *et al.*, 2008). Yet as this paper shall now go on to argue, New Labour's sustained interest in educational ICT can be seen as playing a much wider emblematic role in the party's over-arching drive towards the 'transformation' of the UK public sector along lines fit for a globally competitive economy. In this sense the New Labour ICT agenda between 1997 and 2007 can tell us much about politics and policymaking during this time.

The New Labour ICT agenda: from policy proposals to policy portfolio

Whilst overseeing a succession of policies from the '*Micros in School*' programme in the early 1980s to the '*Education Department Superhighway Initiative*' over ten years after, the Conservative government's approach to education technology was largely piecemeal and non-committal. As such New Labour could not be said to have inherited any substantial form of educational ICT settlement from John Major's outgoing Conservative administration in 1997. As Wild and King observed at the time:

> By the end of the Conservative Government's period of office it was obvious that there was no question of a national [Educational] IT strategy. Obviously this was because there was no internal consistency between what was needed to make the support possible and what had remained available at the time to support the need. (1999, p. 161)

Labour's commandeering of education technology as a distinct policy interest can therefore be seen as an early manifestation of the party's pragmatism—if not canny opportunism—with regards to education policymaking (Power & Whitty, 1999). Whilst in opposition, the Blair administration-in-waiting was certainly quick to recognise education technology as a timely topic, chiming with popular concerns over the 'information superhighway', 'cyberspace' and all things millennial. This pragmatism was extended into the initial development of the party's technology policy commitment, which utilised existing expertise in the area regardless of background or political orientation. Notably, between 1995 and 1997 New Labour commissioned leading figures in the areas of technology, industry and education to fashion a coherent education technology strategy—drawing on the likes of (Lord) Dennis Stevenson, McKinsey consultants and educationalists such as Stephen Heppell to open out the area of education technology as a new line of politics. This preparatory work saw the establishment of education technology as a policy narrative in the making from the 1995 Labour Party conference to the run-up to the 1997 General Election. Perhaps the most significant outcome of these proposals was the conceptual introduction of 'ICT' to the forefront of the education arena as opposed to the previously accepted term of 'IT'. This seemingly minor instance of re-labelling was justified ostensibly in terms of encompassing the emergence of networked computing, although education technologists soon argued that the new term added nothing to the conventional notion of IT which continued to be used in most other countries (see Deeson, 1999). Thus both in terms of substantive policymaking and semantic branding, New Labour was able to claim the area of education technology as its own, just as new technology was becoming of major societal significance. Seemingly out of nowhere, education ICT was established as a freshly minted 'big idea' for Tony Blair's incoming administration and presented as a totem for New Labour's new era of education.

Despite the potential for ICT to become little more than a short-lived policy 'fad', this electoral manoeuvring was followed by a sustained agenda of policymaking throughout the 1998 to 2007 period. Most notably the schools sector was subject to three distinct phases of policymaking: the 1998 to 2002 '*National Grid for Learning*' initiative and associated New Opportunities Fund-supported teacher training programme; the 2002 to 2005 '*ICT in Schools*' drive and associated Curriculum Online and e-learning credit schemes; and the current '*Harnessing Technology*' agenda underpinned by the DfES 2005 'e-learning strategy'. Whilst more autonomous in terms of IT use, the higher education sector was party to the (albeit short-lived) '*UK e-University*' initiative, the HEFCE (2005) strategy for e-learning and, at the beginning of Tony Blair's term in office, the ICT-related proposals of the 1997 Dearing Report. Post compulsory and adult education was subject to a range of initiatives from the *University for Industry* and associated *learndirect* programme to the *UK Online* programme and various other initiatives based around encouraging use of ICTs amongst the adult population. These flagship initiatives were complemented by a succession of smaller programmes and schemes—from the provision of laptop computers to head teachers to the establishment of online content watchdogs.

In practical terms, then, New Labour can claim rightly to have made an unprecedented and sustained political commitment to technology in education since 1998. This is perhaps most evident in their deployment of over £5 billion of funding towards schools' ICT infrastructure alone. In this sense, as Laurillard (2008, p. 1) notes, 'there is no question that government policy [has been] ambitious'. In terms of substantive change the policies were designed to address three areas identified in the framing Stevenson Committee report: namely, the resourcing of education institutions (i.e. hardware resourcing and internet connectivity); the training of teaching staff; and the stimulating and supporting of the production of software and digital content. As with much New Labour policymaking, these areas of action were defined by an array of targets and aims. For instance, the initial *National Grid for Learning* funding was accompanied by a series of targets, such as having all schools, colleges, universities and libraries connected to the internet by 2002, and 75% of teachers and 50% of pupils operating their own email addresses. This funding also encompassed more exhortative targets such as the desire that all teachers 'should generally feel confident, and be competent to teach, using ICT within the curriculum' by 2002; and 'most school leavers should have a good understanding of ICT'. Other ambitions of 'transforming' education institutions and making the UK education system 'fit for the twenty-first century' were regularly espoused (see Selwyn, 2002b). In short, all of these ICT policies were imbued with a range of hopes and agendas above and beyond practical issues of ensuring adequate internet connectivity and providing staff training.

Assessing the educational legacy of the ICT agenda

If the legacy of this policy activity is considered in terms of the government's own stated targets then most of the resourcing targets were met and often exceeded. Certainly in terms of the main aim of introducing ICT into the education system on a widespread basis then New Labour's policies should be seen generally as being successful. Indeed, the substantial increases in funding, resourcing and support of ICT initiated by these policies can be said to have had the outcome of dissipating barriers to ICT use in most if not all education institutions from primary schools to adult learning centres. For instance, the ratio of pupils to computers in primary education fell from 107 pupils per computer in 1985 to around 6:1 in 2007 (BESA, 2007). Similarly, the ratio of pupils to computers in secondary education fell from 61 pupils per computer in 1985 to around 3.6:1 in 2007. Most classrooms are now equipped with interactive whiteboards, curricular guidelines include embedded ICT components, and coursework is dutifully presented by students via Word documents and PowerPoint presentations. Moreover, recent surveys suggest that school teachers are now more technically confident and more likely to make regular use of ICT in their teaching than ever before (Barker & Gardiner, 2007; BESA, 2007). With ICT use now a pedagogic priority in schools and colleges, concerns over lack of access and expertise are certainly felt to be less applicable than before New Labour's rise to power.

Similarly, the aim of creating a sustainable demand for ICT from within the education sector also appears to have been successful. The past ten years have seen education institutions taking control of their own ICT procurement beyond the initial central government funding. Indeed, the rise in UK government funding for ICTs since 1997 has created a large capital infrastructure, which most schools and colleges are now supporting with their own funds (Mee, 2007). The primary sector now spends annually £320 million on ICT hardware and infrastructure alongside £76 million on curriculum software and content. Similarly, the secondary sector now spends annually £281 million on ICT hardware and infrastructure alongside £51 million on curriculum software and content. Moreover, the 1997 to 2007 period saw the establishment of a comprehensive organisational infrastructure dedicated to enhancing ICT use across the education system. As well as official mediating agencies such as *the British Educational Communications and Technology Agency (Becta)* and the *Joint Information Systems Committee (JISC)*, a range of academic, voluntary and private sector organisations also blossomed – from charitable organisations such as *Futurelab* to the education teams of companies such as *Microsoft* and the host of education technology 'labs' based in the university sector. Indeed, the last decade has certainly seen the enhancement of 'the UK's leading reputation for ICT in education' as well as reinforcing the 'fact that it has better figures than most countries in terms of the technological infrastructure for education' (Laurillard, 2008, p. 34).

Yet whilst there is little doubt that the past ten years of New Labour ICT policy-making has had a profound impact on the physical presence of ICT in UK education, the counter-point can nevertheless be made that the much promised technology-based 'transformation' of UK education has failed to materialise. Indeed many of the educational and technological issues that the New Labour ICT agenda purported to address can be said to remain as problematic in 2008 as they were in 1997. This was illustrated in the official admissions towards the end of the Blair administration, for example, that 'only one in six schools and colleges are getting the full benefit of using technology in a truly effective way' (Crowne, 2007), that initiatives such as *UK Online* were making little difference to social inequalities (UK Online, 2007) and that the UK continues to fall behind other comparative countries in ICT skills (Leitch, 2006). Thus despite government assurances that 'we know from the research evidence the difference that information technology can make' (Jim Knight, in Woodward, 2008, p. 2) the fact remains that ICT has failed to substantially alter the nature of UK education as New Labour long had us assume that it would.

The impact of the New Labour ICT agenda has undoubtedly been compromised by a number of practical factors—not least the institutional and organisational factors which beset education technology implementation the world over, such as mitigating curricular and assessment structures, as well as the physical, spatial and temporal constraints of schools, colleges and universities as 'fixed' industrial organisations (see Selwyn, 2007). Above and beyond these perennial factors, the New Labour agenda was also seen to be constrained by the multi-agency management of the initiatives in the UK and the difficulty of securing private sector support (Younie, 2006). Indeed, whilst great play was made of the 'great strength' of public and private expertise and finance (DfEE, 1997) and 'bringing together the best of private sector creativity and the highest standards of public service' (DfEE, 1997, p. 3) the involvement of private sector interests in New Labour's education technology policies has remained inconsistent over the past ten years. Although New Labour continue to talk of 'big, crunchy negotiations' with the IT sector (Jim Knight in Woodward, 2008, p. 2), industry actors remain at best cautious and at worst hostile—as evident in the cessation of the publicly-funded £150 million creation of 'BBC Jam' digital learning content in the face of private sector concerns. As Tim O'Reilly (2007, n.p.) recently commented, 'for an administration keen on the involvement of the private sector in the provision of public services, ICT has not seen the sustained involvement of private concerns'.

Thus the legacy of the New Labour ICT agenda can only be seen as achieving partial success in terms of substantive practical change to the UK education system. In this sense the New Labour agenda would seem to have been unable to transcend the perennial cycle of hype, hope and disappointment which has long characterised the implementation of education technology around the world (Cuban, 2001). As Laurillard (2008, p. 1) recently reflected, 'education is on the brink of being transformed through learning technologies; however, it has been on that brink for some decades now'. Thus the lack of tangible educational transformation in the UK over the past ten years is perhaps unsurprising. It could be argued, however, that to view the New Labour ICT agenda purely in terms of debates over the educational 'effectiveness' of the past ten years' investment is to overlook what should be seen as the real lasting achievement of the New Labour project—i.e. the valorisation and subsequent use of the *idea* of 'ICT' in the face of the rather less impressive *implementation* of ICT. In this sense the distinctive legacy of New Labour's ICT drive should not be seen in practical terms but in ideological terms.

Assessing the ideological legacy of the ICT agenda

Highlighting the emblematic role of the New Labour ICT agenda reflects the contention that the primary under-pinning rationale for such technology-related policymaking is often not as a direct attempt to shape educational technology use *per se*. Instead, as Jensen and Lauritsen (2005, p. 365) note, public sector policies such as the *National Grid for Learning* and the *Harnessing Technology* strategies act 'rather like relay[s] between certain administrative and political practices and a diversity of local initiatives'. In this sense much of the New Labour ICT policy agenda should only be seen as seeking to engineer educational change in an indirect and aspirational manner. In many ways then, the suite of ICT policies under New Labour drive should be seen as a series of tentative steps of releasing some ideas about technological change into the educational domain in the hope that they may stimulate or provoke change. As Jensen and Lauritsen (2005, p. 368) observe, 'there is a package, shiny in its vagueness, of ideas—balls thrown in the air, in the hope that someone will catch them—and formulations that are yet unfulfilled with any practical or even ideal content'. Thus it should be of little surprise that ten years after the *National Grid for*

Learning proposals one finds a gulf between New Labour's lofty global ideals ('moving the education service into the twenty-first century and creating a connected society') and the resulting mundane local actions on the ground (augmenting internet connectivity and developing 'e-safety' protocols). In fact, given the avowedly political nature of the initiatives one would expect fully the realities of ICT change to become ever 'more mundane and compromised' in contrast to the 'grand ideas' of the initial policy documents (Jensen & Lauritsen, 2005, p. 364).

Perhaps the most significant legacy of the New Labour drive has been the ideological rather than practical establishment of 'ICT' within the UK education system. This observation continues Goodson and Mangan's (1996) critique of the ideological underpinnings of 'computer literacy' as it was then being inserted into education institutions throughout the 1980s and 1990s. Here it was argued that computer literacy was a poorly defined and delineated concept, lacking clarity of educational purpose or outcome. Yet Goodson and Mangan argued that the vagueness surrounding the concept was not entirely accidental, nor the mere result of confusion among its proponents. Instead they argued that 'computer literacy' was a largely ideological concept, whose fuzziness and internal contradictions served to mask the social, political and economic agendas it was being used to propagate. Thus as Michael Apple also reasoned:

> the debate about the role of the new technology in society and in schools is not and must not be just about the technical correctness of what computers can and cannot do. These may be the least important kinds of questions, in fact. Instead, at the very core of the debate are the ideological and ethical issues concerning what schools should be about and whose interests they should serve. (2002, p. 442)

In this sense it can be argued that the New Labour 1997–2007 ICT agenda served primarily to establish 'ICT' as a strengthening and updating of the long-standing ideological articulation of 'computer literacy' within the UK education system. Indeed, ten years on one can see how policies such as the *National Grid for Learning* served to establish 'ICT' as a form of consensual discourse in educational arenas—pervasive, widely accepted, and backed by hitherto unseen levels of official authority (Apple, 1990). The pervasive ICT 'world-view' and its continual common-sensical recourse to vague notions of the 'effectiveness' and 'impact' of ICT in the classroom belied the lack of real transformation of the UK education system. More subtly, it also served to obscure the structures of power and real shaping economic and commercial concerns behind the ostensibly bland, neutral face of educational ICT as proposed by New Labour (Sussman, 1997).

In particular, looking back over the 1997–2007 period the articulation of 'ICT' can be seen in at least two related discursive chains—the modernisation of public sector institutions and enhancement of the UK's competitiveness in the global economy. For instance, one can see how New Labour's notion of educational ICT became located quickly within more general notions of modernisation, standards and effectiveness of the public sector. Indeed, as the latter years of the 1990s turned into the initial years of the 2000s, it can be argued that ICT became less of a policy concern in its own right and more a cipher through which educational policy concerns of the day (such as standards, truancy, bullying, parental involvement and so on) came to be expressed. The use of ICT as an ideological vehicle for the reform of the education system along lines of modernisation can be seen clearly in the DfES e-learning strategy which stressed the contribution that ICTs should be making to enhancing educational flexibility, inclusion, productivity and personalisation. In this sense 'ICT' was being used as an ideological vehicle for the government's wider ambitions for the modernisation of education regarding raising attainment, widening participation, increasing personalisation, flexibility, collaboration, staff development and partnerships (DfES, 2005). Moreover, the nature of this modernising project was focused primarily on adapting to the needs of globalisation. As Cole reasoned at the beginning of the Blair administration:

> If globalisation is used ideologically as the *raison d'être* of New Labour economic policy, then modernisation is the conduit through which the policy is introduced. (1998, p. 323)

Indeed, as these latter examples suggest, the argument can be made strongly that rather than reflecting an interest in educational technology *per se*, the New Labour ICT agenda was located firmly within wider prevailing concerns over enhancing competitiveness in a globalising economy and creating a lifelong learning system fit for a successful knowledge economy. Indeed, the framing of ICT in terms of economic reasons and rationales was explicitly laid out in Tony Blair's early description of the combination of education and technology as 'the best economic policy we have' and as a crucial element in making 'the individual and business fit for the knowledge-based economy of the future' (Blair & Schroeder, 1999, p. 2). In this sense it was clear from the outset of the New Labour project that the economic rather than pedagogic significance of ICT was driving and shaping its implementation in the classroom. The economic mandates of New Labour's ICT agenda are to be found throughout all of the policies introduced between 1997 and 2007, not least in the notion that ICT could act as a delayed means of increasing a nation's economic competitiveness in the knowledge-driven economies of the post-industrialised world. As such it can be argued strongly that the ICT agenda was conceived and perpetuated by New Labour as a concerted attempt to change the economic 'mindset' of future workers towards a technologically-based global competition, up-grading the skills base of emerging cohorts of young people and creating the 'workforce flexibility' to counter the threat of a global labour market. In this sense ICTs were appropriated as a ready means though which schools, colleges and universities could fulfil their role as 'core institutions of capitalism' (Garnham, 2000, p. 142).

Conclusions

Although this reading of the ideological appropriation of ICT may not be immediately apparent to many learners or teachers, it is crucial to recognise the constraining nature of these different political and economic influences on what is now being experienced as 'education technology', resulting from the New Labour ICT agenda. Within the narrow construction of ICT as an economic good, the primary functions of technology-using education institutions were not of fostering learning or ensuring equality of opportunity but supporting the reconstruction of the individual worker-citizen and, in particular ensuring the emergence of a 'high-skills' workforce. If educational processes were considered at all, then it was often in restricted terms of a human capital approach towards economic success and efficiency. This leaves ICT positioned firmly within wider economic projects of standardising curricula, improving educational 'standards', widening participation rates in post-compulsory education and increasing levels of 'lifelong learning'. Given the top-down nature of this conceptualisation of education it can now be of little surprise that technology-based teaching and learning in UK education is constructed predominantly in terms of delivery rather than discovery, and that technology-based learners end up in the position of being recipients of pre-packaged curricula. In all, the ICT use in most UK educational institutions is very different from the learner-centred social constructivist and socio-cultural models of technology use idealised by most in the education technology community.

Thus the legacy of the New Labour ICT agenda can be seen as heightening the profile but also limiting the scope of 'ICT' in educational settings. Moreover, there is little reason to expect much change in this situation over the *next* ten years of government, regardless of the outcome of the next general election. Certainly in terms of the politics of education technology it would seem that one of the strongest legacies of the 1997–2007 ICT agenda has been the opening up of ICT as an uncontested policy space. Although there has been recent talk of ICT appearing to be 'falling down the government's agenda' (Dodson, 2007, p. 3), the Gordon Brown government shows no signs of diminishing its commitment to the *Harnessing Technology* agenda—recently proposing ideas for free internet access for under-privileged households and online 'real-time reporting' between school and parents on pupils' lessons, performance and behaviour (Ministerial Taskforce on Home Access, 2008). Similarly the Conservative party has swung from the view in 2005 that 'the Tory party may be many things but it is not an internet party' (Cameron, 2005) to now approaching the internet as 'truly exhilarating, liberating [but] also a challenge' (Cameron, 2008, p. 29). Indeed, the heightened political capital now to be gained from public sector ICT policymaking was evident in Cameron's recent derisory caricature of Gordon Brown as 'an analogue prime minister in a digital age' (*Guardian*, 2008, p. 30). If nothing else, claiming guardianship of the economic-led ideology of educational ICT is now a more prominent and permanent part of the education policy landscape.

Indeed there is little sense of education technology policies being unshackled from wider economic agendas and top-down notions of public sector reform. Investment in education looks set to continue to be based on economic rather than egalitarian and social justice cases for investing in education, with Gordon Brown continuing the Blair mantra that 'the best economic policy is a good education policy' (Beckett & Kingston, 2007). In this sense there is a growing need for the education policy community and other concerned stakeholders to explore alternative ways of truly 'realising the potential of technology'. In particular it would seem appropriate to explore ways of changing the goals of ICT policy-making—i.e. moving the primary motivations away from concerns over global economic transformation and consider the development of genuinely 'educational' policies that seek to implement technology along the lines of teaching, learning or organisational improvement, rather than for ulterior and tangential motives of economy or politics. Although such change in emphasis would require careful thought and a deep re-assessment of educational and political priorities it is clear that maintaining the *status quo* can not be considered as a viable option if viable hopes of technology realising its potential in educational settings are to be sustained. Above all, it is clear that significant changes in policy approaches towards ICT should lie at the heart of efforts to engineer more effective, equitable and perhaps even exciting forms of education in the information age. Whether the legacy of the past eleven years of New Labour's ICT agenda allows this to take place remains to be seen.

Acknowledgements

The author would like to thank the editor, the two anonymous referees and Magdalini Kolokitha for their comments on an earlier draft of the paper.

References

Apple, M. (1990) *Ideology and curriculum* (2nd edn.) (London & New York, Routledge).

Apple, M. (2002) Is the new technology part of the problem or part of the solution in education? in: A. Darder, M. Baltodano & R. Torres (Eds) *The critical pedagogy reader* (London, Routledge).

Barker, R. & Gardiner, J. (2007) *Focus on the digital age: e-learning and e-skills* (London, National Statistics). Available at: www.statistics.gov.uk/downloads/theme_compendia/foda2007/Chapter3.pdf.

Beckett, F. & Kingston, P. (2007) Education notebook, *The Guardian* Education supplement, 26 June, p. 4.

BESA (2007) *Information and communication technology in UK state schools* (London, British Educational Suppliers Association).

Blair, T. & Schroeder, G. (1999) *The third way/die neue Mitte* (London, British Labour Party).

Brown, P. (2007) Tony Blair—a success as Prime Minister? Comments to *Centre for International Relations, International Affairs Forum Roundtable Forum*, May.

Cameron, D. (2005) Interview on the BBC Radio 4 *Today* programme, 28 November.

Cameron, D. (2008) My generation is already adapting to new politics, *The Guardian*, 4 March, p. 29.

Cole, M. (1998) Globalisation, modernisation and competitiveness: a critique of the New Labour project in education, *International Studies in Sociology of Education*, 8(3), 315–332.

Crowne, S. (2007) Keynote speech presented to *Harnessing technology: delivering the future for learners: North East regional conference*, Newcastle, 15 March.

Cuban, L. (2001) *Oversold and underused: computers in the classroom* (Cambridge MA, Harvard University Press).

Dearing Committee [National Committee of Inquiry into the Higher Education] (1997) *Higher education in the learning society: report of the national committee* (London, National Committee of Inquiry into the Higher Education).

Deeson, E. (1999) Communication on information technology, *British Journal of Educational Technology*, 30(4), 369–370.

DfEE (Department for Education and Employment) (1997) *Connecting the learning society, National Grid for Learning* (London, Department for Education and Employment).

DfES (Department for Education and Skills) (2005) *Harnessing technology: transforming learning and children's services* (London, Department for Education and Skills).

Dodson, S. (2007) Local advisors face the axe, *The Guardian*, Education Link supplement, 19 June, p. 3.

Garnham, N. (2000) Information society as theory or ideology, *Information, Communication & Society*, 3(2), 139–152.

Giddens, A. (2007) New Labour—ten years on, *LSE and Progress public debate*, London School of Economics, 9 May.

Goodson, I. & Mangan, J. (1996) Computer literacy as ideology, *British Journal of Sociology of Education*, 17(1), 65–80.

Guardian (2008) Brown's white heat, editorial in *The Guardian*, 20 May, p. 30.

HEFCE (Higher Education Funding Council for England) (2005) *HEFCE strategy for E-learning* (Bristol, Higher Education Funding Council for England).

Hudson J. (2002) Digitising the structures of government: the UK's information age government agenda, *Policy & Politics*, 30(4), 515–531.

Jensen, C. & Lauritsen, P. (2005) Reading digital Denmark: IT reports as material-semiotic actors, *Science, Technology & Human Values*, 30(3), 352–373.

Laurillard, D. (2008) *Digital technologies and their role in achieving our ambitions for education* (London, Institute of Education).

Leitch Review of Skills (2006) *Prosperity for all in the global economy—world class skills* (London, HM Treasury).

Mee, A. (2007) E-learning funding for schools: a policy paradox? *British Journal of Educational Technology*, 38(1), 63–71.

Ministerial Taskforce on Home Access (2008) *Report from the Ministerial Taskforce on Home Access* (London, Department for Children, Schools and Families).

O'Reilly, T. (2007) *Tim O'Reilly on web 2.0 and education: interview with Steve Hargadon*, 26 April. Available online at: www.stevehargadon.com/2007/05/tim-oreilly-on-web-20-and-education.html.

Peckover, S., Hall, C. & White, S. (2008) From policy to practice: the implementation and negotiation of technologies in everyday child welfare, *Children and Society*, 13(6) (forthcoming).

Power, S. & Whitty, G. (1999) New Labour's education policy: first, second or third way? *Journal of Education Policy*, 14(5), 535–546.

Selwyn, N. (2002a) E-stablishing an inclusive society? technology, social exclusion and UK government policy making, *Journal of Social Policy*, 31(1), 1–20.

Selwyn, N. (2002b) *Telling tales on technology: qualitative studies of technology and education* (Aldershot, Ashgate).

Selwyn, N. (2007) Plus ça change, plus c'est la meme chose—considering the probable futures of education technology, in: D. Kritt & L. Winegar (Eds) *Education and technology: critical perspectives and possible futures* (Lanham MD, Rowman & Littlefield).

Sussman, G. (1997) *Communication, technology and politics in the information age* (Thousand Oaks CA, Sage).

UK Online (2007) *Digital inclusion: a discussion of the evidence base* (London, FreshMinds).
Wild, P. & King, P. (1999) Education and IT policy: virtual policy? In: J. Demaine (Ed.) *Education policy and contemporary policy* (Basingstoke, Macmillan).
Woodward, W. (2008) Plan to give every child internet access at home, *The Guardian,* 4 January, p. 2.
Younie, S. (2006) Implementing government policy on ICT in education: lessons learnt, *Education and Information Technologies,* 11(3/4), 385–400.

Tony Blair and the politics of race in education: whiteness, *doublethink* and New Labour

David Gillborn

Introduction

> To those who say where is Labour's passion for social justice,
> I say education is social justice.
> Education is liberty. Education is opportunity. (Tony Blair, April 1997)[1]

> The fact is you can talk to a teacher who will tell you that at the early stages of primary school it is perfectly plain which kids will be going off the rails a few years later. ... The black community—the vast majority of whom in these communities are decent, law-abiding people horrified at what is happening—need to be mobilised in denunciation of this gang culture that is killing innocent young black kids. But we won't stop this by pretending it isn't young black kids doing it. (Tony Blair, April 2007)[2]

An opinion poll marking Blair's ten years as prime minister (PM) revealed an interesting range of views: most respondents said he was 'ineffective' (60%) and 'cannot be trusted' (63%); and yet a majority (51%) also described him as 'likeable as a person' (YouGov, 2007, p. 1). Apparently contradictory reactions and perceptions, such as these, often lead to Blair being seen as an enigma. Someone so concerned with being liked that he was once nicknamed 'Bambi', but who then led his country into a war that many viewed as illegal and literally millions protested against on the streets of London (Hammond, 2004). Certainly Blair's premiership saw many changes: in the ten years that separate the quotations (above) education moved from being seen as *the* doorway to freedom and justice, to eventually become yet another disciplinary device, where 'cohesion' and 'integration' would be defined by the perceptions of the White majority and enforced by the state.

It would be a mistake, however, to imagine that these visible changes reflected fundamental shifts in the underlying policies and priorities of Tony Blair and his governments. In this paper I analyse the place of race and education in the Blairite project from a critical race perspective.[3] I argue that although the rhetorical surface, and the precise policy measures, changed frequently and dramatically during the Blair years, in terms of race equality the essentials of the system remained fairly stable: policy was formulated with White people in mind (usually, but not always, White middle-class people). Core education policies were never properly interrogated for their likely race-specific impacts and, wholly predictably, their outcomes were often racist (in that one or more minoritised groups suffered marked disadvantages in relation to the White majority).[4]

The paper begins with an analysis of the early days of Blair's premiership including the first education proposals and the establishment of the Social Exclusion Unit (SEU). I argue that despite a public commitment to race equality, policy continued to treat race/racism[5] as a peripheral issue and, consequently, exacerbated racist inequalities. Next I consider a period that, initially at least, looks very different: the Stephen Lawrence Inquiry propelled the issue of 'institutional racism' to the top of the news and policy agendas.[6] The experience of the following years, however, suggests that the government's response served a largely cosmetic purpose in wider policy terms. Finally, I consider Blair's conduct at the end of his premiership, when the so-called 'War on Terror' gave a new impetus to popular authoritarian and racist politics.

This analysis, therefore, focuses on New Labour policy and on Tony Blair's own presentation of the core ideas. It is, of course, impossible to definitively separate Blair's personal views and ideas from those of other participants in the policy arena, especially his inner circle of advisers. But it would also be wrong to absolve Blair of responsibility given his stated identity as a 'conviction politician' (Campbell, 2007, p. 129). Wherever possible I draw on Blair's own statements as data that reveal some of the core ideas shaping race and education policy during his premiership.

The early days

> 'Goodbye Xenophobia' (Front page headline, *The Observer*, 4 May 1997)

It is difficult to over-state the sense of widespread relief with which progressive commentators welcomed Tony Blair's election as PM. The headline in that week's

Observer newspaper (above) captured perfectly the sense of epochal shift that many sensed as Blair's 'New' Labour swept away 18 years of Conservative rule with the largest Labour majority in history. Surely now things would be different?

At first sight the signs were positive but, behind the rhetoric, almost immediately a gulf could be detected between, on one hand, the fine words and public sentiment in support of race equality, and on the other hand, a reality where the principal education reforms not only ignored race equality but actually relied on measures that would probably make matters worse.

Just 67 days after taking office Blair's new Government published its first detailed statement of policy intentions and, true to his often-quoted election commitment to make education his first (second, *and* third) priority, the first New Labour White Paper focused on education. In a significant break with the tone of policy under the preceding Conservative administration, *Excellence in Schools* (DfEE, 1997) proclaimed 'the Government's core commitment to equality of opportunity and high standards for all'. The ritual citation of 'standards' (measured in a crude form through national tests and school league tables) was a clear legacy from previous Conservative policy but a focus on equality of opportunity contrasted sharply with the Conservatives' open hostility to the issue; what Kate Myers memorably termed *equiphobia* (Myers, 1990). Under Margaret Thatcher the Conservatives had made sweeping reforms to the system (including the imposition of national testing regimes and the introduction of a statutory 'National Curriculum') all pursued without any meaningful reference to cultural diversity and with complete disregard (often contempt) for the likely consequences for minoritised pupils, parents and communities (see Tomlinson, 2008, ch. 3). '*Colour-blindness*' (an obstinate refusal to consider ethnic diversity despite a wealth of evidence that minorities are *not* sharing equally) was Prime Minister John Major's official policy:

> Few things would inflame racial tension more than trying to bias systems in favour of one colour—a reverse discrimination that fuels resentment. An artificial bias would damage the harmony we treasure. Equality under the law—yes; equality of opportunity and reward—yes. These promote harmony.
>
> Policy must be colour blind—it must just tackle disadvantage. Faced by British citizens, whatever their background might be. (Major, 1997, p. 7)

In a dramatic break with Conservative approaches, Labour's policy documents involved a new emphasis on 'equal opportunities' and an explicit concern with *race* inequalities. *Excellence in Schools* included a section entitled 'Ethnic minority pupils' that referred to raced inequalities in achievement and offered modest commitments to consult on ethnic monitoring and 'best practice' in multi-ethnic schools (DfEE, 1997, pp. 34–35). A year later another significant policy intervention repeated the same pattern: the first report of the new Social Exclusion Unit took education as its theme and, once again, the scale of race inequities was noted (SEU, 1998).

Unfortunately, the symbolic break with colour-blind approaches did not translate into meaningful action. Both the education White Paper and the SEU report discussed race inequalities separately from the rest of the analysis and left the main thrust of policy untouched by any sense of ethnic diversity. Consequently, an understanding of racism and race inequality remained absent from how the principal policy issues were conceived. As a result, policy continued to pursue colour-blind targets (Gillborn, 1997, 1998). Indeed, the principal education reforms threatened to *worsen* existing race inequalities. The SEU report on school exclusions, for example, set targets to reduce the overall number of permanent exclusions but failed to set any race-specific target despite the continuing over-representation of Black students in the official statistics. Similarly, New Labour's distaste for selection *between* schools did nothing to dampen their belief in the utility of selection *within* schools.

In his keynote speech to the 1996 Labour Party Conference, Blair made this commitment:

> No return to the 11-plus. The comprehensive system will stay, modernised for today's world, taking account of children's different abilities but not setting them apart. (quoted in the *Times Educational Supplement*, 4 October 1996, p. 4)

In fact, *setting* children apart is exactly what Blair's education policy did right from the start. The 1997 election manifesto stated:

> We must modernise comprehensive schools. Children are not all of the same ability, nor do they learn at the same speed. That means 'setting' children in classes to maximise progress, for the benefit of high fliers and slower learners alike. (Labour Party Manifesto, 1997, p. 7)

Support for the wider use of 'setting' had been an emerging part of Labour's education policy for some time. Predictably, *Excellence in Schools* had a good deal to say on the subject, including the following version of the history of comprehensive education:

> The demands for equality and increased opportunity in the 1950s and 1960s led to the introduction of comprehensive schools. All-in secondary schooling rightly became the normal pattern, but the search for equality of opportunity in some cases became a tendency to uniformity. The idea that all children had the same rights to develop their abilities led too easily to the doctrine that all had the same ability. The pursuit of excellence was too often equated with elitism. (DfEE, 1997, p. 11)

From the very start, therefore, New Labour accepted commonsense beliefs in ability as a relatively fixed and measurable potential that was best served by separating children on the basis of what the 1997 manifesto called, their 'distinct abilities' (Labour Party, 1997, p. 4). This view was later enshrined in the development of 'Gifted and Talented' schemes, initially as part of the *Excellence in Cities* programme, launched in 1999, but then rolled out nationally. Despite its meritocratic aspirations, antiracists argued from the very start that these policies would deepen existing race inequalities. Decades of research in the US and UK had demonstrated that whenever teachers (the vast majority of whom are White) are asked to rank students according to some measure of ability, motivation, attitude or behaviour, then particular minoritised groups are systematically over-represented in the lowest ranked groups (especially African Americans in the USA and African Caribbeans in the UK) (see Gillborn, 1999). Despite its rhetorical commitment to evidence-informed policy (Whitty, 2006), education policy under Blair refused to hear antiracist warnings and repeated the failures of the past. Dismissing antiracist criticism of the 'Gifted and Talented' measures, for example, the Education Department stated:

> The gifted and talented scheme will identify children by looking at ability, rather than attainment, to capitalise on the talents of the individual child, regardless of ethnic background. (BBC News OnLine, 2002)

Incredibly their own rebuttal demonstrated clearly that the Education Department was working under the familiar but mythic belief that 'ability' and 'attainment' are somehow different (as if 'ability' were some inner quality or potential). In fact, *all* tests (including IQ tests) measure *current* knowledge and, therefore, performance can be raised by tutoring (see Sternberg, 1998; Gillborn, 2008, ch. 5; Stobart, 2008). There is no detectable inner limit to the possible future performance of students. Even where a test is used to *predict* future performance, such as with the popular 'CAT' (Cognitive Abilities Test), all that is being done is that the tester is using past performance to say how students who received that score in the past usually performed later on when they took their GCSEs (Gillborn & Youdell, 2000).

Three years after the initial warning and the official rebuttal (above), the DfES published the first breakdown of 'Gifted and Talented' cohorts by ethnicity. The data showed that White students were the most likely to be identified as 'gifted and talented': the White rate was more than twice that of Black Caribbean children and five times that for their Black African peers (DfES, 2005, p. 36).

The Stephen Lawrence Inquiry

> Looking back now, I am sure that if the government had realised all that would come out of the inquiry, they would not have let it take place. (Doreen Lawrence, 2006, p. 179)

The Stephen Lawrence case is one of the most important episodes in the history of British race relations. Like the wider story of Blair's premiership, the case seemed initially to promise a major step forward in progressive politics, only for time to confound expectations and render the words not merely empty promises but reveal them to be diversionary tactics that hid ever more regressive realities.

Stephen Lawrence was 18 years old when he was murdered in an unprovoked racist attack by white youths in 1993. Stephens's mother and father (Doreen and Neville Lawrence) led a high profile campaign for justice which drew support from diverse sources, ranging from Nelson Mandela—who met them just weeks after the murder—through to the *Daily Mail* newspaper, which publicly accused five men of the killing.[7] In the face of such widespread coverage it was no surprise when 1997's incoming Labour government agreed to an official inquiry, more than four years after the murder.

Much of the inquiry was held in public and the nightly coverage in the news media meant that the catalogue of police errors and racism was broadcast nationally; initially to a sceptical public but eventually to a growing sense of outrage. The swagger of the accused men as they entered the inquiry was especially striking and caused widespread revulsion (see BBC News Online, 1998). When the inquiry report was published (Macpherson, 1999) the revelations about the police's arrogance, incompetence and racism were such that the government *had* to be seen to respond. Every major daily newspaper covered the report in stories that ran across several pages, with headlines repeatedly citing a sense of national shame and the need for change:

> The Legacy of Stephen: Judge's damning report on race murder will change Britain. (*Daily Mail*, 25 February 1991, p. 1)
>
> Stephen Lawrence's legacy: confronting racist Britain. (*The Guardian*, 25 February 1991, p. 1)
>
> A family tragedy, a police force disgraced and a nation shamed. (*The Independent*, 25 February 1991, p. 1)
>
> Nail Them: Mirror offers £50,000 to catch Lawrence killers.
> Damning verdict that shames the nation. (*Daily Mirror*, 25 February 1991, pp. 1, 6)

As the report was published Tony Blair told parliament of his pride in having established the inquiry and proclaimed it to be a turning point in race relations:

> The publication of today's report on the killing of Stephen Lawrence is a very important moment in the life of our country. It is a moment to reflect, to learn and to change. It will certainly lead to new laws but, more than that, it must lead to new attitudes, to a new era in race relations, and to a new more tolerant and more inclusive Britain. (*Hansard*, 1999, cols 380–381).

The following year saw radical changes to the race relations laws. Amendments to the Race Relations Act meant that more than 45,000 public bodies now faced a legal duty to act pro-actively to ensure race equality. The limits of space mean that an exhaustive analysis is not possible here but, unfortunately, the fate of the reforms can be appreciated from even the briefest review of subsequent developments.

In May 2002 the Race Relations (Amendment) Act, passed two years earlier, became active. The new regulations required every state-maintained school to have a written race equality policy; to monitor student achievement and staff appointments for signs of racial bias; and to publicly plan to eliminate race inequality. Incredibly, less than a year later, in January 2003, the then home secretary David Blunkett gave a speech where he argued that 'the slogan created a year or two ago about institutional racism missed the point' (*Guardian*, 2003). In a statement that seemed to betray a total failure to understand the Lawrence Inquiry, and its view of institutional racism as the racist beliefs, actions and processes that disadvantage minoritised people in practice (regardless of intent), Blunkett said:

> It's not the structures created in the past, it's the processes to change structures in the future and it's individuals at all levels who do that. That's why I was so worried about people talking about institutional racism because it isn't institutions, it's patterns of work and processes that have grown up. It's people that make the difference. (*Guardian*, 2003)

The following month provided powerful evidence that the new laws were not having the desired effect. An independent review (headed by Gus John) found that more than a third of English universities were not complying with their legal duties (John,

2003). A few months later a survey for the Commission for Racial Equality (CRE) found that two-thirds of schools had not set any specific goals for improving levels of attainment, despite this being explicitly highlighted in the legislation (Schneider-Ross, 2003). And it was not only schools and universities who were slow to react to their new legal duties on race equality: the entire direction of education policy was revealed as disturbingly colour-blind when a bold new 'Five Year Strategy' was launched (DfES, 2004). Running to 110 pages the document mentioned '*standards*' an impressive 65 times; 'business/es' warranted 36 references; but racism, discrimination (and even the more anodyne 'prejudice') were entirely absent. Just five years after Blair promised 'a new era in race relations …' his government's education plans had apparently jettisoned any concern with race equality and the fight against institutional racism.

Research on the over-exclusion of Black students revealed more cause for concern. Many people assumed that Ofsted inspections would play a key role in ensuring that schools met their race equality duties. In practice, however, it emerged that even when inspection reports included statistics documenting the over-representation of Black students in the school's exclusions, this was *not* identified as an issue that the school needed to address in any follow up action (Parsons *et al.*, 2004).

If the failure of schools, universities, Ofsted and policy-makers to take account of the Lawrence Inquiry could be excused as 'mere' inaction, inattention, or misunderstanding, then 2005 brought unmistakeable evidence that Blair's government was actively stepping back from even the pretence of honouring its commitments to the Lawrence family and to racial justice. In September 2005 the then Home Secretary Charles Clarke decided to disband the Stephen Lawrence Advisory Committee (a group established in 1999 to help take forward the recommendations of the Lawrence Inquiry Report). A couple of months later, in the government's sixth progress report on the Lawrence recommendations, Clarke expressed his personal dedication to race equality, stating '[this] is the first report since I became Home Secretary and I am personally committed to the continuing delivery of this Action Plan' (Home Office, 2005, 3). No further progress reports have ever been published.

The final retreat from Lawrence came in 2007, just weeks before Blair handed the reins to Gordon Brown, when the Government launched a consultation document on a 'Single Equality Bill' which was meant, in the words of the 2005 manifesto, to 'modernise and simplify equality legislation' (Labour Party, 2005, p. 112). A key principle was that:

> The duty is designed to help all public authorities to do what they do better, not stop them operating effectively or weigh them down with bureaucracy. The duty should not lead any public authority to feel it needs to take any action which might be disproportionate to the benefits the action would deliver. (Department for Communities and Local Government, 2007, p. 89)

If enacted, the proposals will remove all the gains made after the Lawrence Inquiry by allowing public bodies to decide which equalities issues are relevant (they may legally decide that 'race' is not a pressing concern) and whether addressing an inequality is actually worthwhile. Consequently, under the proposed new system, even if a school decides that race inequality *is* relevant, it is free to choose not to take action if it judges that the effort is disproportionate to the benefit (see CRE, 2007). At a stroke the new equity proposals would legitimate the racist status quo within the education system.

I have argued elsewhere that the Lawrence case represents a classic example of what critical race theorists have termed '*contradiction-closing cases*' (see Bell, 1985; Delgado, 1998; Gillborn, 2008). These cases occur when there is a contradiction between, on one hand, the state's preferred narrative of society as overwhelmingly meritocratic and just, and on the other hand, some event or series of events that reveal the true extent of real material inequality and disadvantage as systemic phenomena. The contradiction is closed by reforms that *appear* to have addressed the inequality but actually leave the situation pretty well unchanged. Indeed, things might even be *worse* because the celebrated case now stands as evidence of the state's benign nature. In this case the far-reaching requirements of the Race Relations (Amendment) Act appeared to have addressed the institutional racism that was thrown into stark relief by the Stephen Lawrence Inquiry. But the effect was almost entirely cosmetic.

Popular authoritarianism and the 'War on Terror'

> It would be a mistake to underestimate the effect of 9/11 on the psychology of the Government or Tony Blair. (John Prescott, deputy prime minister 1997–2007, 2008, p. 305)

Blair's overall legacy is irrevocably tied to his military actions in Iraq and Afghanistan. In the field of race and education these actions had particular resonance because the so-called 'War on Terror' had dramatic consequences for policy in relation to minoritised people in general, and Muslims in particular (Gillborn, 2008; Tomlinson, 2008). The level of popular authoritarianism grew markedly stronger after the London bombings of July 2005. Rather than try to review the full scope of this trend, it is revealing to examine one particularly important example: Blair's vision of *integration*.

As 2006 drew to a close Blair, who had already stated his intention to step down the following year, made a series of keynote statements intended to cement his legacy and ensure policy continuity (regardless of whoever succeeded him). His statement on 'the duty to integrate' made headline news and seemed designed to project a tough, no-nonsense image. Television news broadcasts repeatedly showed the same sound-bite from the end of the speech:

> Our tolerance is part of what makes Britain, Britain.
> So conform to it; or don't come here. (Blair, 2006) [8]

'In other words', as Karen Chouhan (2006) noted, 'Britain's tolerance is based on intolerance'. The sound-bite was typical of the disciplinary nature of the entire speech. The word *duty/duties* appeared ten times in the body of the speech and was used in a cavalier fashion that belied both the complexity of the issues and the very real fear and intimidation that Muslim communities increasingly experienced

(Bhatia, no date). The speech also announced a new restriction on would-be migrants that echoed the decades old obsession with the English language (Gillborn, 2008; Tomlinson, 2008) but actually went further than any previous policy phase by insisting that the language now become a *prerequisite* for citizenship. Typically, however, the measure was presented, not as a restriction, but as a requirement of 'cohesion' and 'justice':

> It is a matter both of cohesion and of justice that we should set the use of English as a condition of citizenship. In addition, for those who wish to take up residence permanently in the UK, we will include a requirement to pass an English test before such permanent residency is granted. (Blair, 2006)

This policy is even more restrictive and racist (likely to disproportionately hit non-White applicants) than anything enacted in the original decades of assimilationism in the 1950s and 1960s. This same authoritarianism was later solidified in government guidance on school uniforms. Although the guidance made no direct reference to the veil, it stated that 'if a pupil's face is obscured for any reason, the teacher may not be able to judge their engagement with learning, and to secure their participation in discussions and practical activities' (DfES, 2007). The document found support in *The Sun* newspaper whose headline read 'Veil Ban on Kids' (20 March 2007, p. 1).

Conclusion

> Doublethink ... to hold simultaneously two opinions which cancelled out, knowing them to be contradictory and believing in both of them ... (George Orwell, *Nineteen Eighty-Four*)[9]

Early in Blair's premiership I remember presenting a seminar paper on racism and education policy. I talked about Thatcherite constructions of the nation and showed a slide of the following quotation:

> ... consider a thousand years of British history and what it tells us. The first parliament of the World; the Industrial Revolution—ahead of its time; an Empire, the largest the World has ever known, relinquished in peace. The invention of virtually every scientific device of the modern World. Two World Wars in which our country was bled dry, in which two generations perished, but which in the defeat of the most evil force ever let loose by man showed the most sustained example of bravery in human history. This is our nation.

The audience shook their heads in disgust. They were appalled at such a chauvinistic construction of the past. Some laughed at its supreme arrogance: 'The invention of virtually every scientific device ...'. Others scoffed at the idea that the British Empire had been relinquished at all, let alone that independence had been peacefully gifted: what about the numerous Slave Rebellions, the Irish revolt and the American War of Independence? But the sense of shared outrage was replaced by shock when I revealed that the speaker was not Margaret Thatcher but Tony Blair (during his address to the Labour Party Conference in 1996). One audience member simply rejected the possibility out of hand. The words might have appeared on a web-site, they argued, but there was no way that *Tony* would actually say such a thing. The following day I sent them an audio recording of the segment and offered to copy them a video of the entire speech.

The incident is significant for many reasons. It reveals that a crude, even jingoistic, nationalism was always present in Blair's politics but went unnoticed for many years. In his resignation speech on 10 March 2007 he stated:

> This country is a blessed nation.
> The British are special.
> The World knows it; in our innermost thoughts *we* know it.
> This is the greatest nation on Earth.

Blair's brand of nationalism is especially important because it illuminates his government's failure to understand the nature of the racism revealed by the Stephen Lawrence Inquiry. Despite its radical rhetoric, New Labour never moved beyond a superficial notion of equal opportunities; education policy simply could not accept that many fundamental assumptions that appear commonsensical (such as the nature of 'ability') are actually deeply implicated in the creation and legitimation of racist educational inequality. Hence the colour-blind targets, the failure to rigorously enforce the amended race legislation, and the love affair with setting and 'giftedness'. Hence, the same PM who celebrated the Lawrence Inquiry could (less than a decade later) happily stereotype youth crime as a facet of a racialised sub-culture:

> What we are dealing with is not a general social disorder; but specific groups or people who for one reason or another, are deciding not to abide by the same code of conduct as the rest of us. This came home to me when, at the recent summit I held on knife and gun crime, the black Pastor of a London church said bluntly: when are we going to start saying this is a problem amongst a section of the black community and not, for reasons of political correctness, pretend that this is nothing to do with it. (Blair, 2007)

For all the high hopes on his election and the rhetorical commitments to equity, therefore, Tony Blair was not an enigma, and he broke no mould. Blair represents the latest in a long line of White politicians who have shaped education policy in the interests of White people. The principal beneficiaries of his policies have been White children (the *only* ethnic group to improve their GCSE performance every year during his reign (Gillborn 2008)). When the façade of a non-racist Britain was shattered by the Lawrence Inquiry his government produced radical new laws but soon moved on and failed to enforce them. And in the post 9/11 context of his later years in power, Blair proved himself all too ready to support moves against Islamic dress in school and the further demonisation of Black young men as a criminal presence in society. From a critical race perspective, Blair's premiership is a story of broken promises, betrayed trusts, and overwhelming continuity with the racist history of the country he described as 'the greatest nation on Earth'.

Notes

1. Quoted in the *Times Educational Supplement*, 18 April 1997, p. 6.
2. Quotation is from Blair (2007).

3. Critical race theory (CRT) is a radical tradition that emerged from US legal studies in the 1980s and is increasingly influential in educational studies (see Delgado & Stefancic, 2001).
4. I use the term 'minoritised' to refer to those race/ethnic groups who are rendered a power minority by the operation of White assumptions and interests, regardless of their numerical representation at a global, national, local or school level.
5. The social construction of 'race' differences is *always* associated with raced inequities. Consequently the notion of 'race' inevitably carries racist consequences (see Leonardo, 2002).
6. The Stephen Lawrence Inquiry defined institutional racism as 'the collective failure of an organisation to provide an appropriate and professional service to people because of their colour, culture, or ethnic origin. It can be seen or detected in processes, attitudes and behaviour which amount to discrimination through unwitting prejudice, ignorance, thoughtlessness and racist stereotyping which disadvantage minority ethnic people' (Macpherson, 1999, p. 321).
7. For a detailed account of the Lawrence case, including an itemised chronology, see Gillborn, 2008, ch. 6.
8. An uncorrected text was published on the 10 Downing Street website: http://www.pm.gov.uk/output/Page10563.asp#content (accessed 10 December 2006). All quotations here are taken from the text *as delivered*: broadcast on BBC News Online at http://news.bbc.co.uk/1/hi/uk_politics/6219626.stm (accessed 16 January 2007).
9. Orwell (1949, p. 35).

References

BBC News Online (1998) Lawrence murder inquiry re-opens. Available online at: http://news.bbc.co.uk/1/hi/uk/123068.stm (accessed 20 January 2008).

BBC News Online (2002) Racism warning over curriculum plans. Available online at: http://news.bbc.co.uk/1/hi/education/1867639.stm (accessed 5 November 2005).

Bell, D. (1985) Foreword: the Civil Rights Chronicles (The Supreme Court, 1984 term), *Harvard Law Review*, 99, 4–83.

Bhatia, S. (no date) The stares in the London Underground. Available online at: http://www.cobrapost.com/documents/Staresshekharbhatia.htm (accessed 5 September 2006).

Blair, T. (2006) *The duty to integrate: shared British values*. The full speech is available online at http://news.bbc.co.uk/1/hi/uk_politics/6219626.stm (accessed 16 January 2007).

Blair, T. (2007) *Callaghan Memorial Speech*, 11 April 2007. Available online at: http://www.number-10.gov.uk/output/Page11472.asp (accessed 20 April 2007).

Campbell, A. (2007) *The Blair years: extracts from the Alastair Campbell diaries* (London, Hutchinson).

Chouhan, K. (2006) Letter from the Black London Forum and the 1990 Trust. Available online at: http://www.blink.org.uk/docs/CEHR_priorities.pdf (accessed 22 January 2007).

CRE (Commission for Racial Equality) (2007) *CRE Briefings on Discrimination Law Review: equality duties* (London, CRE). Available online at: http://www.cre.gov.uk/downloads/dlr_paper3.pdf (accessed 8 August 2007).

Delgado, R. (1998) Rodrigo's committee assignment: a sceptical look at judicial independence, *Southern California Law Review*, 72, 425–454.

Delgado, R. & Stefancic, J. (2001) *Critical race theory: an introduction* (New York, New York University Press).

Department for Communities and Local Government (2007) *Discrimination Law Review: a framework for fairness: proposals for a single equality bill for Great Britain.* A consultation paper (London, Department for Communities & Local Government).

DfEE (Department for Education and Employment) (1997) *Excellence in schools,* Cm 3681 (London, The Stationery Office).

DfES (Department for Education and Skills) (2004) *Five year strategy for children and learners* (London, DfES).

DfES (Department for Education and Skills) (2005) *Ethnicity and education: the evidence on minority ethnic pupils* (London, DfES).

DfES (Department for Education and Skills) (2007) *Guidance to schools on school uniform related policies,* 20 March (London, DfES).

Gillborn, D. (1997) Racism and reform: new ethnicities/old inequalities? *British Educational Research Journal,* 23(3), 345–360.

Gillborn, D. (1998) Racism, selection, poverty and parents: New Labour, old problems? *Journal of Education Policy,* 13(6), 717–735.

Gillborn, D. (1999) Race, Nation and Education: New Labour and the New Racism, in: J. Demaine (Ed.) *Education policy and contemporary politics* (London, Macmillan), 82–102.

Gillborn, D. (2008) *Racism and education: coincidence or conspiracy?* (London, Routledge).

Gillborn, D. & Youdell, D. (2000) *Rationing education: policy, practice, reform and equity* (Buckingham, Open University Press).

Guardian (2003) Blunkett dumps 'institutional racism'. Available online at: http://www.guardian.co.uk/race/story/0,11374,874613,00.html (accessed 14 January 2003).

Hammond, M. J. (2004) From Bambi to Stalin: the politics of control and power within the further education sector under New Labour. Paper presented at the *Discourse, Power, Resistance Conference: Global Issues, Local Solutions Conference,* University of Plymouth, 5–7 April.

Hansard (1999) Prime Minister's Questions, 24 February, cols 379–387. Available online at: http://www.publications.parliament.uk/pa/cm199899/cmhansrd/vo990224/debtext/90224-20.htm#90224-20_spmin0 (accessed 3 May 2007).

Home Office (2005) *Lawrence steering group: 6th Annual Report* (London, Home Office).

John, G. (2003) *Review of race equality policies and action plans: HEFCE-funded higher education institutions* (Manchester, Gus John Partnership).

Labour Party (1997) *New Labour: because Britain deserves better* (London, Labour Party).

Labour Party (2005) *Britain forward not back: Labour Party manifesto 2005* (London, Labour Party).

Lawrence, D. (2006) *And still I rise: seeking justice for Stephen* (London, Faber & Faber).

Leonardo, Z. (2002) The souls of white folk: critical pedagogy, whiteness studies, and globalization discourse, *Race Ethnicity and Education,* 5(1), 29–50.

Macpherson, W. (1999) *The Stephen Lawrence inquiry.* Cm 4262-I. (London, The Stationery Office). Available online at: http://www.archive.official-documents.co.uk/document/cm42/4262/4262.htm (accessed 2 May 2007).

Major, J. (1997) *Britain—the best place in the world.* Text of a Speech to the Commonwealth Institute, 18 January (London, Conservative Central Office).

Myers, K. (1990) Review of 'Equal opportunities in the new era', *Education,* 5 October, 295.

Orwell, G. (1949) *Nineteen eighty-four* (Harmondsworth, Penguin).

Parsons, C., Godfrey, R., Annan, G., Cornwall, J., Dussart, M., Hepburn, S., Howlett, K. & Wennerstrom, V. (2004) *Minority ethnic exclusions and the Race Relations (Amendment) Act 2000.* Research Report 616. (London, Department for Education & Skills).

Prescott, J. (2008) *Prezza: my story: pulling no punches* (London, Headline).

Schneider-Ross (2003) *Towards racial equality: an evaluation of the public duty to promote race equality and good race relations in England and Wales* (London, Commission for Racial Equality).

Social Exclusion Unit (1998) *Truancy and school exclusion report by the Social Exclusion Unit.* Cm 3957 (London, SEU).

Sternberg, R. J. (1998) Abilities are forms of developing expertise, *Educational Researcher,* 27(3), 11–20.

Stobart, G. (2008) *Testing times: the uses and abuses of assessment* (London, Routledge).

Tomlinson, S. (2008) *Race and education: policy and politics in Britain* (Maidenhead, Open University Press).

Whitty, G. (2006) Education(al) research and education policy making: is conflict inevitable? *British Educational Research Journal,* 32(2), 159–176.

YouGov (2007) *Ten years of Tony Blair: YouGov/Daily Telegraph survey results.* Available online at: http://www.yougov.com/uk/archives/pdf/TEL070101010_3.pdf (accessed 20 December 2007).

Making teaching a 21st century profession: Tony Blair's big prize

John Furlong

Introduction

> After decades of drift, decisive action is required to raise teaching to the front rank of professions. Only by modernisation can we equip our nation for the new century. I hope you will join us in meeting this challenge. (Tony Blair, DfEE, 1998a, Foreword)

Throughout Tony Blair's ten years in office, his aspiration to reform the teaching profession was a remarkably consistent one. The aim, set out originally in a Green Paper (DfEE, 1998a) just one year after he came to office, was to change the ground rules of what teacher professionalism actually meant in order to harness that professionalism closely to the government's own educational reform agenda. This, I will argue, is what he meant by making teaching a '21st century profession'.

In analysing this aspect of Tony Blair's educational policy, this paper has a number of different aims. First, in order to throw some light on why reforming the teaching profession was seen as such a high priority for successive administrations, I begin by briefly considering Tony Blair's broader 'campaign' on educational reform, its underlying motivations and its key policies. In the main part of the paper I document the range of different strategies that the Blair government used in harnessing the teaching profession to the achievement of those policies. I then go on to consider the consequences for the teaching profession, both positive and negative, of these significant reforms. And finally, I conclude by considering something of Tony Blair's legacy in this field, both in the UK and particularly internationally.

Education: a national campaign

One of the most distinctive features of educational policy throughout the Blair years was that it was of such high priority. It was a 'national campaign' spoken about on many occasions with passion and commitment.

The reasons are not hard to find. As Blair himself said in his introduction to the Green Paper *The Learning Age*: 'Education is the best economic policy we have' (DfEE, 1998b). In other words, education under Tony Blair moved from being a *social* policy to an *economic* policy. In a world of intense competition between nations, as Lauder *et al.* (2007) have recently argued, education increasingly plays a key role. National prosperity, social justice and cohesion are all seen to rest on the shoulders of education, on the creation of a highly skilled workforce with the knowledge, enterprise and insights required to attract the global supply of high-skilled, high-waged employment.

And the distinctive strategy to be used by new Labour was that its educational reforms were strongly centrally directed. As Michael Barber, who in the early years of the Blair government was responsible for the implementation of New Labour's school reforms, has stated:

> A lot of people within the system say we went too far too fast and should have made more effort to get buy-in. I personally don't believe that. We had to demonstrate that you could do large-scale, system-wide reform quickly. (Barber, 2006, p. 7)

Education, then, was for Tony Blair of the highest national importance. That is why those reforms had such a high priority; and that is why teaching had to become a '21st century profession'—teacher professionalism had to be harnessed in a way that would ensure that centrally led reforms were a success.

The need for a 'New Professionalism'

When, in 1998, Tony Blair launched the Green Paper *Teachers: meeting the challenge of change* he described it as 'the most fundamental reform of the teaching profession since state education began' (DfEE, 1998a). Although the Green Paper was intended to begin a process of consultation, it was clear from the very beginning that the *status quo* was not an option.

For a government bent on fundamental, centrally driven educational reforms, there were a number of problems with the teaching profession. The first concerned the supply, retention and quality of new teachers, something that had been a constant worry for British governments since the 1970s. Such concerns, whether real or imagined (See *et al.*, 2004; Gorard *et al.*, 2006), pointed to the need to devise strategies to improve the attractiveness of teaching as a career.

Another perceived difficulty was that teachers as a professional group were largely undifferentiated both in the tasks that they undertook and in the rewards they were offered. In terms of contemporary workforce planning this was seen as an inefficient use of the education system's most costly resource; it was also seen as having a negative impact on the attractiveness of teaching. If the government was going to invest in the schools' workforce and improve retention rates, then roles and responsibilities as well as working practices had to be reformed.

A further difficulty concerned the nature of professional knowledge. On the one hand, because teachers traditionally worked in isolation, and had few opportunities to learn from each other, their professional knowledge was seen as highly personalised, even idiosyncratic. On the other hand, such 'collective' or 'codified' professional knowledge that was available was largely based in universities. As a result, it was seen as highly theoretical and abstract and largely irrelevant to the day-to-day needs of practising teachers. Continuing professional development (CPD) therefore needed fundamental reform, with responsibility moved away from higher education and based more firmly in the schools themselves, but working within national frameworks that would define 'best practice'.

But beyond these problems, more important than any of them, were concerns about teachers' perceived lack of accountability. Even before he came into government, Tony Blair was explicitly invoking an earlier Labour Prime Minister, Jim Callaghan (Blair, 1996), to argue the need for teachers to be far more accountable to their schools, their parents and communities, and, above all, to the government. And if that meant challenging traditional notions of professional autonomy, then so be it.

From the very start, therefore, the Blair government was confident that all of these issues needed addressing in the development of a 'new professionalism' relevant to the 21st century. That was the vision announced in the original Green Paper of 1998 and that vision remained remarkably consistent throughout Tony Blair's years in office. However, as we will see, some aspects of the new professionalism took longer to achieve than others.

More teachers, better teachers

The first major raft of changes concerned the supply and quality of new teachers. Here, initial teacher training (ITT) had a key role to play. The pay of newly qualified teachers was increased so that it was more in line with other occupations for new graduates—a 10% increase in starting salaries resulted in a 30% increase in applications (McKinsey report, 2007). A series of bursaries to attract teachers into subjects such as mathematics and science also significantly helped to address recruitment in these traditionally hard to recruit subjects.

Considerable attention was also paid to the public image of the profession. Here the Teacher Training Agency (TTA) (later to be re-branded as the Training and Development Agency for Schools (TDA)) was given a major role to play through a high profile television advertising campaign and the employment of a range of marketing and recruitment techniques used in business.

But the aim to recruit more teachers was also matched by the pressure to increase the quality of new entrants. Throughout the Blair years, the TTA and Ofsted maintained their pressure on providers of initial training to develop rigorous quality assurance systems with penalties for underperforming training providers (Furlong, 2005). Nationally agreed entry requirements and nationally defined 'standards' for the award of qualified teacher status were also put in place; these have been regularly updated to keep in line with changing government definitions of what 'good teaching' involves. (For the latest iteration see TDA, 2007.)

One further strategy relevant to increasing both the supply and quality of new entrants into teaching has involved diversifying teacher recruitment—attracting older applicants, perhaps those with family responsibilities as well as career changers, into teaching. There has also been an increasing acceptance that teaching may not be 'a career for life'—an approach exemplified by the Teach First programme, designed to attract 'high flying' graduates into the profession for a few years. In short, over the Blair years there was a progressive and significant diversification of the system. By 2008 there were 36 different ways to enter the teaching profession in England. Significantly, a number of these new routes were created to be undertaken 'on the job'; currently some 18% of all new recruits enter through an 'employment based system' such as the Graduate Teacher Programme and Teach First.

Overall, therefore, the system of initial teacher training in England was given a major role to play in the 're-tooling' of the teaching profession. Indeed, the work of the TTA in reforming ITT and securing teacher supply has been claimed by ministers as one of the Labour government's success stories (Clarke, 2004a; Kelly, 2005). The numbers of newly qualified teachers in post did increase significantly (by a total of 36,000), as did, according to Ofsted, the overall assessed performance of new teachers (Bell, 2005).

A more differentiated workforce

Another important element of the reform has been the development of a more differentiated workforce—a greater emphasis on leadership and opportunities for promotion, with appropriate pay rewards, as well as a greater use of different types of classroom assistants and support staff—through what has been called 'workforce remodelling'.

The greater emphasis on school leaders was a constant throughout the Blair years. Whatever the political agenda of the day, ministers turned to 'strong and effective leaders' to drive through changes (see for example Jacqui Smith on the Primary Numeracy and Literacy Strategies (Smith, 2005), Charles Clarke on the 'Personalisation' agenda (Clarke, 2003) or Beverley Hughes on 'Every Child Matters' (Hughes, 2007)).

These leaders were headteachers, whose responsibilities and financial rewards increased substantially in the Blair years and, in support of such leaders, the government also established a new body—the National College of School Leadership.

But there was also an emphasis on other forms of leadership—Advanced Skills Teachers, Secondary Heads of Department. As Charles Clarke put it in 2004:

'leadership should be in the culture of a school, in the behaviours of all its staff' (Clarke, 2004b). In short, there should be a more differentiated teaching force than in the past with more opportunities for advancement, matched by what was called a 'modern pay scale'—greater awards but linked to appraisal and the achievement of personalised targets. In line with these ideas, in 1999, the government launched the 'Fast Track Teaching Programme' (NCSL, 2008) to support teachers in their early careers to take on such senior leadership roles more quickly.

Yet differentiation did not only mean more senior positions, it also meant making far more use of classroom assistants and different forms of technical support. Held out in the original 1998 Green Paper as a reward to the profession for accepting performance related pay (which I discuss below), was the promise to diversify staffing structures within schools, thereby freeing up teachers to focus on their core tasks of teaching and learning. The package included a commitment to the devolution of routine tasks such as chasing absentees and record keeping, a limit on the requirement to cover for absent colleagues, and a guaranteed 10% planning and preparation time. In addition there was a commitment significantly to increase the numbers of all types of support staff—from bursars to Higher Level Teaching Assistants —with skills in specific areas of expertise.

By 2006, nine years after the original Green Paper proposals, education minister Jacqui Smith was able to claim that the new scheme was starting to show benefits with almost 270,000 support staff in schools—double the number in 1997 (Smith, 2006).

A more 'managed' professionalism

However, as I indicated above, far more important and, indeed, far more controversial than any of the above reforms, was the aspiration on the part of Tony Blair's government to develop greater control over the *content* of teacher professionalism. Rather than leave it to individual teachers and schools to set their own objectives, the aim was to find ways of ensuring that teachers' day-to-day practice, and indeed their aspirations (both for themselves and for their schools), were focused as explicitly as possible on government defined policies. In a long drawn out process of 'shadow boxing' with the profession, higher salaries, better opportunities for promotion, more classroom assistants and the long awaited establishment of a General Teaching Council—all these were offered in return for what the government really wanted: the acceptance of a more 'managed' professionalism, where professional goals and standards would become closely aligned to current policy concerns of the government.

Interestingly, the focus of this newer, managed professionalism evolved constantly during Tony Blair's ten years in office. In the early years, it was mainly focused on overall standards of measured achievement at Key Stage (KS)4 and in primary schools in relation to the literacy and numeracy strategies; then a similar approach was extended into secondary schooling with the KS3 strategy. Later, the Every Child Matters agenda came to the fore which, some would argue (Andrews, 2008), tended to muddle the early focus on achievements in literacy and numeracy. And in its most recent iteration, policy has moved on again, with its focus on the 'personalisation' of learning. But while the government's substantive agenda changed, its aspiration to develop more direct control of teachers' professionalism remained constant. If literacy and numeracy were to be improved, if the personalisation of learning was to be achieved, then ways had to be found of ensuring that teachers, throughout the length and breadth of the country, took on these government objectives as their own.

This distinction between the *aims* of educational reform and the *means* of achieving them is bluntly set out by the McKinsey Report (2007) on improving school systems internationally; it drew significantly on the experience of the Blair government's reforms:

> The first part of the challenge [in educational reform] is to define what great instruction looks like. That task is ... relative[ly] straightforward from a system management perspective: [it involves] ... finding the best educators and giving them the space to debate and create a better curriculum and pedagogy. The second part of the challenge ... is much more complex: giving thousands of teachers the capacity and knowledge to deliver that great instruction reliably, every day across thousands of schools, in circumstances that vary enormously from one classroom to the next—and all of this with very little oversight. (p. 29)

Targets, strategies and national training schemes

> Targets are an essential part of the process for raising standards. They show what we need to achieve, provide a clear focus for improvements, particularly in teaching and learning, and are an important means of measuring progress. (DfES, 2003, p. 1)

Target setting was central to Tony Blair's strategy throughout his period of office, with targets themselves changing, becoming more challenging and more sophisticated over time. Specific targets were linked to evolving policy priorities. For example, the 1997 White Paper, *Excellence in schools* (DfEE, 1997), was closely linked to the Literacy Strategy. These targets were to be based on data generated by the national tests, with schools required to set their own targets for improvement, based on information about similar schools. The White Paper also announced legislation that would give local authorities power to intervene in schools that had problems, although local authority funding was itself threatened if those same authorities failed to produce adequate development plans.

By 2000, David Blunkett, the then Secretary of State for Education, was announcing the extension of both the Literacy and Numeracy Strategies into the secondary years (the Key Stage 3 Strategy) with further extensions into science and ICT in subsequent years (Blunkett, 2000).

In the establishment of this approach to 'managing' through targets, developments in ICT had a key role to play. From its very inception, ICT was seen as an essential ingredient in the new professionalism. The vision of a 21st century professional was of a teacher fully conversant with how to integrate new technologies into their teaching strategies; new technologies, it was argued, would open up a wealth of opportunity for pupils to take greater control of their own learning. Yet despite the constant mantra of the 'transformative possibilities' of new technologies for teaching and learning and despite massive investment, their real impact on day-to-day classroom practice remained elusive during the Blair years. On the other hand, the impact of ICT on school data systems, which allowed individual pupil, teacher and school targets to be monitored, was immense.

As a DfES advisory document put it in 2003,

> To have any meaning in the classroom, targets must reflect what teachers know about individual children. The information available in the Pupil Achievement Tracker (PAT) about the progress that children can make between different Key Stages will help schools to set appropriate targets for individual children. (DfES, 2003, p. 1)

By 2006, more sophisticated data and statistical techniques had been developed and were allowing the government to extend its definition of what was meant by 'unacceptably low performance' of schools; targets now had to include notions of 'value added' and 'contextual value added' where individual students' prior attainment and school context were to be taken into account. As a result of these new metrics, local authorities were required to issue warning notices to schools 'even if the absolute level of attainment is apparently satisfactory' (DCSF, 2007, para. 45).

Targets, standards and CPD

The Blair years also saw a new approach to continuing professional development (CPD). For example, the introduction of the national strategies for literacy, numeracy and KS3 were linked to an ambitious national programme of training, managed by the Standards and Effectiveness Unit at the DfEE, with a direct link to the Prime Minister. The Unit worked with a national team of advisers who in turn trained local literacy consultants who in their turn trained staff in all primary schools in their areas.

More broadly, CPD was moved from a system focusing on personal professional learning to a system designed primarily to support performance management (DfEE, 2001). That change was based on three distinct principles. First, there was an emphasis on schools themselves taking responsibility both for identifying development needs and for providing support themselves—by the 'best practitioners'—with a greater emphasis on mentoring and coaching. (See for example speech by Secretary of State Ruth Kelly at the launch of the TDA (Kelly, 2005).)

Underlying this vision was the expectation that professional development was a constant; it should be part of the everyday activities of all teachers but clearly set in the context of specific schools. Schools were expected to make the decisions about what their priorities were, informed by 'accurate management and performance data'.

A second principle was that such school-focused and school-based professional development should be linked to national strategies and developed within an increasingly explicit national framework. When it was re-launched in 2005, one of the TDA's first tasks was to develop a set of professional standards expected of classroom teachers in England, throughout their career: Qualified Teacher Status, teachers on the main scale, teachers on the upper pay scale, Excellent Teachers and Advanced Skills Teachers (TDA, 2006).

The third and final principle was that CPD should be unequivocally linked to the pursuit of standards, a point made clear by education minister, Jacqui Smith, in 2005 in a speech to the General Teaching Council for England:

> Professional development needs to be linked to performance management and school development priorities ... And I think it's only right that we should keep a relentless focus on standards .., We know the principal way to spread best practice across the whole school system is when teachers can learn from others teachers and schools can learn from other schools. (Smith, 2005)

Linking standards to appraisal and performance related pay

This linking of CPD to targets and standards brings us to the final strategy pursued during the Blair years to develop a more 'managed' professionalism; that was the introduction of performance related pay (Mahony & Hextall, 2001). Originally foreshadowed in the 1998 Green Paper, performance related pay took nearly the whole of Tony Blair's time in office to achieve.

What was on offer was a significant increase in pay, but only if the profession signed up to a performance related pay agreement with annual appraisal and with a career grade 'threshold'. Performance management for teachers, as David Miliband, the minister responsible for introducing the changes, said in 2004, had to be based on 'challenge, rigour and hard evidence' (Miliband, 2004). Appraisal therefore had to include assessment of classroom performance through observation and, in an explicit attempt to link the appraisal system to broader government objectives, it had to include an individualised analysis of pupil progress. Pupil progress also had to be taken into account in the setting of individual targets for each teacher; at least one of those targets had to be directly linked to the school's pupil performance targets.

In addition, in an attempt to deal with the issue of under performance, a career threshold was introduced; to pass it, teachers had to demonstrate that they had consistently achieved new national standards in their classroom performance.

Given the controversial, indeed radical, nature of these proposals, it is not surprising that they were resisted—particularly by the National Union of Teachers. In the end the performance pay agreement ('Raising standards and tackling workload: a national agreement') was not finally signed until 2003 and did not come fully into effect until 2005. However, through it, the government established a strong mechanism for ensuring that, in the future, teachers would remain focused on centrally defined agendas—expressed as 'standards'.

Consequences and legacies

In academic circles, there has been much speculation about the consequences of the new professionalism; on the 'intensification' of teachers' work (Hargreaves, 2003), and what Ball has dramatically called 'the terrors of performativity' (Ball, 2003). There has also been a renewed interest in teacher stress and teacher burnout (e.g. Troman & Woods, 2001). But the truth is that the majority of teachers did adapt; they have not resigned despite the 'terrors' of performativity. Indeed, throughout Tony Blair's ten years in office, the numbers of new teachers entering the profession increased year on year and, with the exception of the NUT campaign on performance related pay, it was, by and large, a period of industrial peace. Salaries increased, the General Teaching Council was successfully launched and rapidly gained widespread acceptance (even if its remit was much more narrowly proscribed than some had originally hoped (Kirk, 2000)) and the media campaign did seem to have had some impact on the public image of the profession.

And yet, at another level, it is clear that the profession did change but perhaps in more subtle and one might suggest in more profound ways. First, it changed in relation to the nature of professional knowledge. The Blair years saw the acceleration of the move, begun under the previous Conservative government, towards a technical rationalist approach to professional knowledge. As I have discussed elsewhere (Furlong, 2005) the growing marginalisation of higher education in initial teacher education, and particularly in in-service education (with its overwhelming emphasis on the networking of 'what works'), has served to narrow still further the forms of professional knowledge available to the teaching profession. Research and theoretical knowledge remain important—in some ways they are more important than ever before, but they are forms of knowledge that are only relevant to policy makers and their expert advisers. As the McKinsey report states so baldly, once the educational experts have worked out what 'excellent instruction is', then it is the task of government to 'roll out' that policy for all teachers. In this way, knowledge has been 'hollowed out' and the opportunities for individual teachers themselves to engage with that research, to debate the nature or value of proposed forms of 'excellent instruction', has been systematically marginalised and removed.

In turn, this 'hollowing out' of knowledge has had major implications for professional identities. As Beck and Young (2005) argue, for generations professional identities have centred in a particular kind of relationship to knowledge, a relationship which was centred on what Bernstein termed 'inwardness' and 'inner dedication'. It is this, Beck and Young argue, that is profoundly threatened by the rising tide of marketisation, external regulation and the audit culture. In this world, strong attachments to particular views of teaching, to particular educational values, can come to be seen as dysfunctional, even pathological. Instead, what contemporary policy is seeking, they suggest, is the 'endlessly re-trainable employee' as policies change and develop over time—from literacy and numeracy, to Every Child Matters, to 'personalisation'.

Two recent large-scale studies would corroborate this view. One by Day and others (Gu & Day, 2007) was a longitudinal government funded study of 300 teachers across 100 schools in England. What the authors document is that many teachers in the early 2000s did indeed face substantial professional challenges; they experienced the intensification of performativity and a challenge to some of their traditional educational values. However, the authors suggest that, for most teachers, what helped them adapt to this new environment was their sense of vocationalism, their personalised commitment to their students, even if they disagreed with the broad thrust of the education policy they were required to implement.

Another study—the Teacher Identities Project (Moore *et al.*, 2002)—analysed the experiences of 70 practising teachers and eight school principals in nine London schools. The most significant finding of the study was that most teachers described themselves as both pragmatic and eclectic; few teachers declared themselves as either wholesale supporters or rejecters of government reforms in education; almost all talked of the ways in which they had modified previous practice to 'bring it in line' with current policy, or had found ways of incorporating current policy into a largely unaltered continuing practice.

The point about eclecticism and pragmatism, the authors argue, is not that it is new. 'What is new is for teachers to adopt the terms so ubiquitously and enthusiastically at the moment' (p. 561). Is this, they ask, leading to the de-politicisation of the teaching profession in which healthy educational debate is being replaced by an all-pervasive politics of compromise?

In truth, such studies remain speculative; it will perhaps take far longer for the real consequences of the impact of Tony Blair's 'new professionalism' to be fully appreciated. But what of the political legacy of his mission to modernise the teaching profession? Is there indeed a legacy? Domestically, much will hang on the outcome of the next general election and, at the time of writing, this is hard to predict. If elected, the Conservative party could well shift their interest back to initial teacher education, focusing strongly on raising the 'quality' of new entrants to the profession: abandoning the BEd and making work-based training the 'default' mode of entry into the profession (Policy Exchange, 2008). Such moves, it is hoped, would increase the attractiveness of the profession to high quality applicants; it would of course further weaken the links between the profession and research and theoretical-based knowledge.

But if Tony Blair does have a political legacy in this field it is, I would suggest, in the international arena. In recent years, two major international and highly influential reports have been published on how to develop 'high performing' education systems—the OECD report, *Teachers matter* (2005) and the McKinsey report, *How the world's best performing school systems come out on top* (2007). Both see the management of the teaching profession as key and both have been significantly influenced by the last ten years of experience in England.

And there is evidence that this message is now widely accepted internationally. A recent special edition of *Teachers and Teaching* that I have co-edited (Furlong *et al.*, 2008) examined a range of countries: the USA, Australia, continental Europe, Namibia, Singapore and Scotland. Virtually all report similar policy aspirations on behalf of their governments; they too now want to follow Tony Blair's lead and ensure that teacher professionalism is closely aligned with national educational policy. (The only real exception is Scotland (Menter & Hulme, 2008) although see also Reynolds on Wales in this volume (Reynolds, 2008).)

Over the ten years of his term of office, it is clear that Tony Blair was indeed successful in his ambitious attempts at reform. At the end of his term of office, there were more teachers, and they were more diverse in terms of their backgrounds than before; they were also better paid, better supported by teaching assistants and, if the

McKinsey report is right, more highly regarded. But they were also much more managed than in the past. Powerful mechanisms had been put in place to ensure that teachers, in their day-to-day practice, did indeed conform to the centrally prescribed policy agendas and strategies, whether or not they agreed with them.

Of course, whether or not such a model of professionalism is the most appropriate one for the 21st century is a very different question. Interestingly, Singapore, with one of the world's most successful modern economies, is now, despite having a centrally controlled education system, taking a different view. There, as Hogan and Gopinathan (2008) suggest, the government has moved beyond technical rationalist solutions. Instead, it is searching for a more open form of teacher professionalism that will support the development of 'thinking schools' which might become the test-beds of inquiry and innovation necessary to maintain Singapore's position in the global economy. It could well be that, if these messages are taken seriously, in a few years Tony Blair's narrower, technically rationalist vision of professionalism will come to be seen as anything but the most appropriate model for the 21st century.

Acknowledgments

Thanks are due to Alaster Douglas, Alan Slater and Cerys Furlong.

References

Andrews, R. (2008) Ten years of strategies, *Changing English,* 15(1), 77–85.

Ball, S. (2003) The teacher's soul and the terrors of performativity, *Journal of Education Policy,* 18(2), 215–228.

Barber, M. (2006) *Education reform lessons from England: an interview with Sir Michael Barber* (Washington DC, Education Sector). Available online at: http://www.educationsector.org/analysis/analysis_show.htm?doc_id=344385.

Beck, J. & Young, M. (2005) The assault on the professions and the restructuring of academic and professional identities: a Bernsteinian analysis, *British Journal of Sociology of Education,* 26(2), 183–197.

Bell, D. (2005) *Annual report of Her Majesty's Chief Inspector for schools, 2003–5* (London, Ofsted).

Blair, T. (1996) Speech given at Ruskin College, Oxford, 16 December.

Blunkett, D. (2000) Raising aspirations in the 21st century. Speech to the *North of England Education conference,* Wigan, England, 6 January.

Clarke, C. (2003) Speech to *National College of School Leadership conference for new headteachers,* QE2 Conference Centre, 13 November.

Clarke, C. (2004a) Speech at the *TTA Corporate Plan Launch,* 29 March.

Clarke, C. (2004b) Speech to *NASUWT Annual Conference,* Llandudno, 14 April.

Day, C. & Gu, Q. (2007) Variations in the conditions for teachers' professional learning and development: sustaining commitment and effectiveness over a career, *Oxford Review of Education,* 33(4), 423–443.

DCSF (Department for Children, Schools and Families) (2007) *Statutory guidance on schools causing concern* (London, DCSF).

DfEE (Department for Education and Employment) (1997) *Excellence in schools (White Paper)* (London, DfEE).

DfEE (Department for Education and Employment) (1998a) *Teachers: meeting the challenge of change* (London, DfEE).

DfEE (Department for Education and Employment) (1998b) *The learning age: a renaissance for Britain* (London, DfEE).

DfEE (Department for Education and Employment) (2001) *Learning and teaching: a strategy for professional development* (London, DfEE).

DfES (Department for Education and Skills) (2003) *Target setting Key Stage 3 and 4 – 2004–6: DfES guidance* (London, DfES).

Furlong, J. (2005) New Labour and teacher education: the end of an era, *Oxford Review of Education,* 31(1), 119–134.

Furlong, J., Cochran Smith, M. & Brennan, M. (2008) (Eds) Politics and policy in teacher education: international perspectives. Special edition of *Teachers and Teaching: theory and practice,* 14(4/5).

Gorard, S., See, B. H., Smith, E. & White, P. (2006) *Teacher supply: the key issues* (London, Continuum).

Hargreaves, A. (2003) *Teaching in the knowledge society: education in the age of insecurity* (New York, Teachers' College Press).

Hogan. D. & Gopinathan, S. (2008) Knowledge management, sustainable innovation and pre-service teacher education in Singapore, *Teachers and Teaching: Theory and Practice,* 14(4/5) forthcoming.

Hughes, B. (2007) School leadership and the Every Child Matters. Speech to the *National College of School Leadership governing Council,* 5 November.

Kelly, R. (2005) Speech at the *Training and Development Agency for Schools launch,* Westminster Central Hall, London, 17 October.

Kirk, G. (2000) The General Teaching Council for England, *School Leadership and Management,* 20(2), 235–246.

Lauder, H., Brown, P., Dillabough, J.-A. & Halsey, A. H. (2007) Introduction: the prospects for education: individualisation, globalisation and social change, in: H. Lauder, P. Brown, J.-A. Dillabough & A. H. Halsey (Eds) *Education, globalisation and social change* (Oxford, Oxford University Press).

Mahony, P. & Hextall, I. (2001) *Reconstructing teaching: standards, performance and accountability* (London, Routledge).

McKinsey report (2007) *How the world's best performing school systems come out on top (McKinsey Report).* Available at: http://www.mckinsey.com/clientservice/socialsector/resources/pdf/Worlds_School_Systems_Final.pdf.

Menter, I. & Hulme, M. (2008) Is small beautiful? Policy making in teacher education in Scotland, *Teachers and Teaching: Theory and Practice,* 14(4/5) forthcoming.

Miliband, D. (2004) Performance management: higher standards, higher status. Speech to the *British Performance Management Conference,* Bournemouth, 26 January.

Moore, A., Edwards, G., Halpin, D. & George, R. (2002) Compliance, resistance and pragmatism: the reconstruction of schoolteacher identities in a period of intensive reform, *International Studies in the Sociology of Education,* 12(1), 195–212.

NCSL (National College for School Leadership) (2008) http://www.ncsl.org.uk/fasttrack-index.

OECD (Organisation for Economic Co-operation and Development) (2005) *Teachers matter: attracting, developing and retaining effective teachers* (Paris, OECD).
Policy Exchange (2008) *More good teachers* (London, Policy Exchange).
Reynolds, D. (2008) New Labour, education and Wales: the devolution decade, *Oxford Review of Education,* 34(6), 753–765.
See, B. H., Gorard, S., White, P. & Roberts, K. (2004) Teacher demand: crisis, what crisis? *Cambridge Journal of Education,* 34(1), 103–123.
Smith, J. (2005) How can we make our best even better? Speech to *Conference of the General Teaching Council for England and London University Institute of Education,* 23 June.
Smith, J. (2006) Speech to *Association of Teachers and Lecturers, Annual Conference,* Gateshead, 12 April.
TDA (Training and Development Agency) (2006) *Professional standards: why sit still in your career?* (London, TDA).
TDA (Training and Development Agency) (2007) *Professional standards for teaching from September 2007* (London, TDA).
Troman, G. & Woods, P. (2001) *Primary teachers' stress* (London, Routledge).

Beyond tuition fees? The legacy of Blair's government to higher education

Ingrid Lunt

Introduction

The now famous mantra of 'education, education, education' applied mainly to the school and nursery sector where the New Labour 'brand' can be seen most clearly. According to one commentator,

> for most of [Blair's] time in office universities took a back seat to more pressing educational concerns, as successive public spending settlements demonstrated. (O'Leary, 2007)

Yet despite its predominant focus on schools and nurseries, the Blair government produced a plethora of initiatives, statements and policies concerning Higher Education (HE) in its ten-year period. According to Brown (2005) 'there have been no fewer than 28 policy pronouncements since 1997', and these were followed by at least a further 15 before the Blair handover.

The direction for the New Labour government's initiatives for HE was initially set by the publication of the Dearing Report (NCIHE, 1997) in July 2007, shortly after the landslide election victory that brought Tony Blair to Downing Street. Although formally commissioned in 1996 by the Conservative government, the Committee of Inquiry had been agreed by both major political parties in recognition of the 'sense of crisis in UK higher education' (Watson, 2007) whose urgency had been emphasised by the Vice Chancellors' 'revolt' in autumn 1995 and their threat in January 1996 to introduce top-up fees in response to the absence of additional public funds. This called for a fundamental debate over the nature, purposes and in particular funding of the higher education sector.

A number of wider pressures provided the context for the Dearing Committee of Enquiry. The major expansion of student numbers that took place between 1987 and 1997, when the age cohort participation rate more than doubled from around 15% to 33%, had resulted in a serious funding crisis, since the amount paid by government to universities per student (the 'unit of resource') had been effectively halved. The shift to a mass system and the abolition of the 'binary divide' (the differentiation between polytechnic institutions and universities in the UK in the period between 1965 and 1992) had created less certainty as to the nature and purpose of UK higher education. The pressures of increasing global competition and the wider imperatives of globalisation, and the growth of the so-called 'knowledge economy' created pressures for an already stretched system. These were also a part of the context which shaped the Blair government's approach to HE, and which made it almost inevitable that there would be some continuity in approach with the Conservative government. In fact, according to Ball (2001), a number of major continuities were the result of global trends rather than 'Labour aberrations', and the principles of 'choice and competition', 'autonomy and performativity' and 'centralisation and prescription' were part of a much bigger global picture.

The New Labour inheritance

The Blair government inherited a Higher Education system which faced a number of major challenges. First, the shift from an élite to a mass HE system, decreased public funding and consequent challenges to the financing of universities, and, second, the perceived need to respond to a competitive global economy coupled with the belief in the link between the economy and the knowledge and skills of the labour force, the so-called 'high skills economy' and the 'commodification' of knowledge. However, these challenges were not unique to the UK, and, as Scott (1995) suggested, 'HE systems in all developed countries are being transformed by the same pressures in similar ways'.

In the UK all three major parties supported expansion of student numbers and the Conservative target of participation by one-third of the age cohort had been achieved by 1997. However, this expansion had not succeeded in reducing class inequalities and appeared to have very significantly benefited young people of middle-class background (Scott, 1995; and see Wolf, 2002; Lawton, 2005), while reaching proportionately fewer working-class young people.

Expansion of HE was accompanied by serious under-funding and a significant fall in the 'unit of resource', such that, according to Dearing (2007), 'on the basis of government plans at the time we were appointed, the unit of resource would have halved in 25 years' (p. 175). According to then Secretary of State David Blunkett

(Blunkett, 2000), funding per student had fallen 36% between 1989 and 1997, during which time the student population had more than doubled. A controversial strategy to address the funding of mass higher education already introduced by the Conservatives was the gradual replacement of the student maintenance grant with loans to be repaid after student graduation.

In addition, a mass higher education system raised fundamental questions about the nature and purpose of the university, a question already raised by granting former polytechnics university status in 1992, which brought together institutions with very different histories, purposes, student bodies and missions. The New Labour inheritance has been summarised succinctly as:

> the Tory years were remembered in universities largely for budget cuts and under-funded expansion. ... Labour was inheriting an over-stretched higher education sector that was in urgent need of renewal. (O'Leary, 2007)

The Blair Government's vision

Early on, Blair signalled a very different direction from that taken by the traditional Left. In making a commitment to redefine radical left-of-centre policies Blair sought to combine social justice with economic prosperity, an aspiration which was reaffirmed in his 2001 Manifesto as 'an even stronger bond between the goals of economic progress and social justice'. However, it was already clear early on that Blair aimed for 'a modern welfare system' based on 'the market', 'choice', 'efficiency', 'standards'.

These terms suggest a clear continuity with the right-of-centre and neo-liberal policies pursued by the Conservatives over the previous government, and a number of authors have commented on the continuity between the Conservative government and New Labour policies (see for example Power & Whitty, 1999; Ball, 2001; Tomlinson, 2001; Whitty, 2002; Lawton, 2005; Jenkins, 2007). As pointed out by Tomlinson:

> much continuity derives from an acceptance and elaboration of Tory reforms post-1988; indeed a pursuit of some of these policies passed the point that Tory ministers had been willing to go. There was an acceptance of the Conservative faith in choice and competition, with education developing as a market commodity driven by consumer demands ... and fuelled by league table publication. (2001, p. 85)

Thus, New Labour adopted the so-called Third Way aiming to combine equity and social justice with competitiveness and market policies. Whitty (2002) has pointed out that in its espousal of the Conservative tenets of choice and diversity, 'as education appears to be devolved from the state to an increasingly marketised civil society, consumer rights will prevail over citizen rights' (p. 87), while Barber (2007, p. 22) emphasised that the so-called reform of public services placed Blair 'firmly on the side of the consumer'.

The New Labour vision for Higher Education included a number of strands as part of its 'universal agenda'. Higher Education was to contribute to Britain's competitive edge in the global market by producing and disseminating economically productive knowledge. The belief that a knowledge-based economy requires more and more highly qualified employees endorsed a continued commitment to increasing the total number of students and within that the overall proportion of graduate students. The requirement that Britain's HE should compete and stand among the top world-class universities meant a focus on further developing the research capacity and output of universities. Economic and financial imperatives implied the creation of incentives for alternative (to the state) modes of funding higher education, and further drives for quasi-privatisation and entrepreneurial activity. In addition, the vision included a firm commitment to widening participation and greater social inclusion. But there remained the big political question of who should pay for continued expansion of higher education.

The Dearing Report

The Dearing Committee had been set up by the Conservative government with the following ambitious terms of reference:

> To make recommendations on how the purposes, shape, structure, size and funding of higher education, including support for students, should develop to meet the needs of the United Kingdom over the next twenty years, recognising that higher education embraces teaching, learning, scholarship and research. (NCIHE, 1997, p. 3)

The Report made a large number of far-reaching recommendations concerning expansion of student numbers (especially at the higher national certificate and diploma (sub-degree) levels), widening participation, increasing public funding on HE, the introduction of a graduate contribution to tuition costs, an emphasis on enhanced professionalism in teaching and expanded quality arrangements.

The Committee was constrained by 'the urgency and complexity' of its task (Barnett, 1999) and by the tensions implicit in the context of its creation. Perhaps most importantly, it was expected to provide solutions to the challenge of the financing of higher education and to find a politically acceptable way of introducing a student contribution to tuition fees (Brown, 2005). It is this issue for which Dearing is largely remembered and it is this issue which proved to be the most contentious for the new Labour government, faced by the urgent political question of how to fund mass higher education.

The Dearing Committee recommended that individual students (who were the beneficiaries of university education) should meet part of the costs of full-time higher education when they could afford to, through income-contingent repayment of loans after graduation, and also that grants should be restored to support those from low-income families. However, having initially rejected the Dearing recommendation in favour of a means-tested up-front tuition fee, the Blair government was forced to 'embrace it, after much turbulence and loss of political face, six years later' (Brown, 2005, p. 25). Indeed, commenting on the Blair government, O'Leary (2007) suggests that:

> higher education provides one of the enduring mysteries of Tony Blair's 10 years in office. Why, when his mantra of 'education, education, education' focused so tightly on schools

> and nurseries, did he risk the future of his administration on a half-hearted reform of university funding? Whether through misjudgement, stubbornness or genuine radicalism, his proposals for top-up fees came closer than foundation hospitals, trust schools or even the war in Iraq to bringing a premature end to his premiership. (p. 468)

According to Watson (2007), with the one major exception of tuition fees mentioned above, the Blair government implemented most of the recommendations, and certainly the broad thrust, of the Dearing report.

Government initiatives for Higher Education 1997–2007

'New Labour Mark 1', as Watson (2007) refers to the first term, was spent mainly on implementation of the Dearing recommendations. In February 2000, towards the end of the first term, David Blunkett set out the New Labour vision for the 'future direction of higher education' in his speech delivered at Greenwich University (Blunkett, 2000). This was the first articulation of the New Labour vision for higher education, and set out 'what have become the main themes of New Labour's engagement with higher education' (Brown, 2005): (i) the crucial role of HE in relation to the new global economy; (ii) the need for genuine diversity of higher education institutions rather than each trying to do everything; (iii) the need for universities to forge alliances and collaborative ventures both with each other and with business and other partners; (iv) the target of at least half of the 18–30 year-olds in some form of higher education by 2010; (v) the need to widen participation in higher education and support social inclusion; (vi) the importance of quality and accountability.

The speech announced a number of specific new initiatives some of which were carried forward, while its language clearly reflected the New Labour 'brand' of 'global competitiveness', 'markets', 'targets', 'performance measures', 'value for money', 'choice ... and genuine diversity', 'new alliances with the private sector', and students as 'critical consumers'. At the same time, higher education was to be a 'potentially powerful instrument of social justice' (Blunkett, 2000, para. 66). In expressing the government's economic and instrumentalist objectives, and its attempts to combine social justice with market competition, the speech set out the 'New Labour Mark 2' vision for the future of higher education.

This vision was endorsed in the Labour Party second term election manifesto in 2001, which reinforced Blair's 1999 commitment to the ten-year target of 50% of 18–30 year-olds entering higher education, and its second term vision was set out in the White Paper of 2003 (DfES, 2003a). In the foreword, Charles Clarke identified three major policy objectives: extending expansion of higher education to students of all backgrounds, increasing efforts in harnessing knowledge to wealth creation and thus enhancing competitiveness, and making the system for student support fairer.

The White Paper set out an ambitious vision, with proposals for enhancing six areas: research excellence; links between higher education and business; the quality of teaching and learning; further expansion towards the goal of 50% participation rate by 2010; widening access to higher education in order to address the continued social class gap in entry to higher education; and encouraging universities to access new funding streams to supplement government funding.

Research funding was to be increased, though concentrated in a smaller number of institutions; links between higher education and business were to be encouraged by targeted funding (e.g. the Higher Education Innovation Fund HEIF), and by an increased role for Regional Development Agencies (RDAs); the status of university teaching was to be enhanced through additional funding and the introduction of Centres of Excellence for Teaching and Learning (CETLs), and more information for students; the commitment to increase access and participation in HE was to be boosted by the introduction of two-year Foundation degrees; the social class gap in entry to higher education was to be addressed by restoring grants for students from lower income families, abolishing up-front fees for all and introducing 'top-up' fees, and by requiring universities to draw up an Access Agreement in return for introducing variable fees, and providing incentives for universities to attract students from non-traditional backgrounds; universities were to be encouraged and helped to raise endowments and other sources of private funds. It is clear that the proposals of the White Paper were driven to a large extent by an economic imperative, and a belief that market policies could be applied to the HE sector, and an increasingly instrumental approach to higher education.

The proposals gave rise to a number of dilemmas and paradoxes which illustrate some of the tensions evident in New Labour education policy (Brown 2003). The first and most enduring tension is that caused by expansion of student numbers and a perceived need to contain costs. A second dilemma reflects the government's commitment to 'choice and diversity', yet with the inevitable hierarchy which institutional 'diversity' is likely to create, with a small number of research-led 'top' institutions, and a number of 'teaching only' institutions. The final dilemma concerns the nature and extent of 'access' and widening participation and the potentially exclusionary or exclusive nature of UK Higher Education, or the trade-off between excellence and equity.

Funding of mass higher education has been, arguably, the biggest challenge for the Labour government. Almost equally challenging has been the commitment to widening participation and fair access which was pursued through an initiative launched in March 2003 shortly after the White Paper (DfES, 2003b). This included proposals to create an Office for Fair Access (or 'access regulator'), and linked universities' ability to charge variable tuition fees to an access agreement committing them to use additional funds raised through fees for bursaries and financial support for students, outreach work to schools, and milestones by which to measure progress towards the goal of widened participation.

The Higher Education Bill was introduced in January 2004 and became law as the Higher Education Act 2004 in July that year. Its main provision was the implementation of the White Paper proposals for student funding and the introduction of 'top-up' or variable tuition fees up to £3000 from 2006 which universities were permitted to introduce provided that they sign up to an 'Access Agreement' with the new Office for Fair Access (OFFA). The fees provision was accompanied by a system of student loans (no student would be required to pay fees up-front), means-tested grants, and university bursaries.

The Blair legacy

Much of the Blair legacy for the period 1997–2007 had a sense of inevitability. Much of the direction had been set by the previous Conservative government and articulated in the Dearing report. However, major initiatives pursued by the Blair government in its second term result from the government's attempts to maintain a simultaneous commitment to a marketised higher education system and a policy of widening participation.

The marketisation of HE begun under the Conservatives has increased (Brown, 2006), reflecting the model of consumption and 'consumers' as a major theme in the New Labour 'modernisation of public services'. Ranking of universities in international league tables has increased explicit competitiveness, while universities compete for students who are seen as customers using 'consumerist levers' (Naidoo & Jamieson, 2005) to enhance their choice and control over the educational process, for example through student satisfaction surveys. Throughout the period, there has been an emphasis on the importance of international students who now make a significant contribution to the British economy (and to other aspects of British life in fostering international relations), with a steady increase in their numbers, in particular at postgraduate level. Targets for international student recruitment have been set since 1999 with the Prime Minister's first Initiative on International Education (PMI1) which aimed to position the UK as a global leader. This was followed in 2006 by PMI2 with further recruitment targets and a focus on the international student experience and strategic partnerships and alliances, couched in the discourse of 'a competitive edge for the UK product in an increasingly crowded market place'. The UK remains second to the USA in terms of market share of international students, although the UK percentage share is increasingly threatened by high tuition fees, perceptions of quality, and the use of English language for teaching by other European universities, and the impact of the Bologna Process in Europe. In future this share may in addition be threatened by countries such as China and India developing their own high quality provision.

Competition to maximise their income leads universities to seek new 'markets' and to reorient themselves to the student-customer so that 'new forms of "delivery" and consumption of HE are being created that can result in learning becoming increasingly fragmented and combined in novel ways with no internal coherence' (Ball, 2008, p. 23, and see Ball, 2007). Thus, the changed relationship between students ('purchasers') and universities ('providers') has led to a change in the student orientation to learning and knowledge, and a 'commodification' of knowledge (or 'services') and 'fragmentation' into 'modules' or 'credits' which may be 'purchased' and transferred, or 'cashed-in' at other institutions. As 'higher education is increasingly seen as an industry for enhancing national competitiveness and as a commodity that can be sold in the global marketplace' (Naidoo, 2003, p. 250) universities are under pressure to adopt principles of value for money, cost-minimisation, flexibility and quality enhancement. Thus, as part of its model for public service reform, the government has used New Public Management (NPM) approaches to performance management and customer choice, using market incentives and customer choice to increase efficiency and quality (Shattock, 2008). There are questions as to how far this 'commodification' of knowledge may affect academic standards, and indeed in what ways the shift to mass higher education at all levels may have an impact on standards of Bachelor, Masters and indeed Doctorate degrees.

As part of a much more prescriptive and centralised system of higher education, there has been a major shift in the nature of the doctorate, driven in large part by the government through the Research Councils. Thus the doctorate now includes prescribed training in research methods and in so-called generic and transferable skills, emphasising employability as 'doctoral graduates are understood as investments in national economic infrastructure and harnessed in the service of a global and increasingly competitive knowledge economy' (Lee & Boud, 2009). This orientation is also evident in the Research Councils' increasingly targeted and strategic approach to funding of research, and in the Government's Strategy for Science and Innovation which aims to ensure UK competitiveness in research and innovation, through the Science and Innovation Investment Framework setting out targets for the decade 2004–2014.

Marketisation (and the government's explicit commitment to 'diversity' of institutions) have led to increased differentiation and potential stratification of universities, as the use of performance indicators and metrics such as the Research Assessment Exercise (RAE) implies research selectivity and research funding concentrated in fewer universities; while the expansion of degree awarding powers to colleges of higher education and in 2006 to colleges of further education led to 'research-intensive' universities and 'teaching-only' institutions.

Despite the commitment to increasing participation, the participation rate among 17–30 year-olds rose by just 0.6% between 1999–2000 and 2006–2007 from 39.2% to 39.8% (*Times Higher Education Supplement*, 17–23 April 2008). Perhaps more worryingly, the total increase in participation rates masks a considerable variation by social class, reflecting the potential tension or trade-off between excellence (élite) and equality (mass) in the HE sector. It still appears to be the case that 'British higher education has become a mass higher education system in its public structures, but remains an élite one in its private instincts' (Scott, 1995, p. 2). This trend is perhaps reflected in the significant increase in post-graduate numbers. According to Watts and Bridges (2006), participation rates of those from lower socio-economic groups remains low in part because it is unclear in what way young people from these groups benefit from higher education, and how far the benefits outweigh the costs (and see Wolf, 2002; Blandon & Machin, 2004). A number of writers have also pointed out the effects of traditional debt aversion of certain groups of young people, and despite the creation of access agreements and bursaries, marketisation and competition between institutions have the potential to undermine policies to widen participation (Morley & Aynsley, 2007). Although the introduction of Foundation Degrees in 2001 was announced as a means to increase and widen participation in higher education through a new two-year more vocationally relevant qualification, they have met with mixed success, and have done little to widen participation.

Financing of mass higher education remains the biggest challenge for governments, and the Blair government leaves a mixed legacy. Despite a number of U-turns concerning tuition fees during the course of the period, it is clear that the direction introduced by the 2004 Education Act will continue, with differential fees likely to increase, and students as 'beneficiaries' of higher education required to make an increasing contribution to costs as state funding reduces. UK universities have become increasingly dependent on international student fee income, as one of a diverse range of income streams which are required to supplement the dwindling state funding.

Competition between universities has been influenced by a highly complex and comprehensive system of academic quality regulation, audit and monitoring (e.g. RAE, QAA Institutional Audit and subject benchmarking) such that institutional diversity is combined with a certain standardisation (Tight, 2006) which encourages 'performativity' and an instrumental approach. Throughout the Blair government and following Dearing recommendations has been the attempt to enhance the quality of and attention to university teaching. This commitment was followed up in the 2003 White Paper which announced the creation of the major and extensive initiative Centres for Excellence in Teaching and Learning (CETLs) which were approved in 74 universities in 2005 with funding of £315 million over five years, representing HEFCE's largest ever single funding initiative in teaching and learning. Professionalisation of HE teaching has also been promoted by the creation of the Higher Education Academy (HEA), formed in 2004 from a merger of the Institute for Learning and Teaching in Higher Education (ILTHE), the Learning and Teaching Support Network (LTSN) and the TQEF National Co-ordination Team (NCT) and the introduction of teaching qualifications for teachers in HE.

Finally, the Blair legacy has had different effects across the UK as a result of devolution and the creation of the Scottish Parliament and the National Assembly for Wales in 1999. Student funding was a major issue in the first Scottish elections in 1999, with the result that there was no introduction of undergraduate tuition fees. Although Scottish universities have diverged more significantly from the system in England and Wales (and Scotland has long had responsibility for its own education system), both countries have evolved an increasingly national system responsive to perceived national needs and reflecting national ideology (Paterson, 2003; Gallacher, 2006; Rees & Taylor, 2006).

Conclusion

Blair's legacy to Higher Education is a highly marketised HE system, in which global competitiveness has been the major driver. Although the age participation rate has not increased significantly over the period, student funding remains a major challenge, as does the challenge of widening participation. University competitiveness has been driven both through the RAE, and through the 'purchaser/provider' model which implies students as 'customers' and the commodification of knowledge and skills. Incentives and targets have driven universities' behaviour in relation to international student recruitment (also an important source of revenue), student bursaries and support, research activities and knowledge transfer initiatives. Competition and league tables are gradually leading to differentiation and stratification of universities, in part driven by the government's commitment to diversity, and in part affected by the diverse needs of the enlarged student body. Universities struggle to balance 'blue skies research' with 'useful' and applicable research in response to government initiatives such as the UK Strategy for Science and Innovation, while the tension between expansion of undergraduate and postgraduate student numbers reflects fundamental dilemmas of academic provision. Teaching and learning have a higher profile in the sector. Although the age participation rate is slowly increasing, there remains a concern that this continues to exclude young people from lower socio-economic classes. The New Labour agenda of enhanced global competitiveness appears to have had a more significant impact on universities than its ideological commitment to social inclusion and equity while leaving fundamental challenges inherent in developing and financing a mass higher education system.

Acknowledgement

I am very grateful for the helpful comments of two anonymous reviewers.

References

Ball, S. (2001) Labour learning and the economy: a 'policy sociology' perspective, in: M. Fielding (Ed.) *Taking education really seriously: four years' hard labour* (London, RoutledgeFalmer).

Ball, S.J. (2007) *Education plc. Understanding private sector participation in public sector education* (London, Routledge).

Ball, S.J. (2008) *The education debate* (Bristol, Policy Press).

Barber, M. (2007) *Instruction to deliver* (London, Politico's Publishing).

Barnett, R. (1999) The coming of the global village: a tale of two inquiries, *Oxford Review of Education*, 25(3), 293–306.

Blandon, J. & Machin, S. (2004) Educational inequality and the expansion of UK Higher Education, *Scottish Journal of Political Economy,* 51(2), 230–249.

Blunkett, D. (2000) Speech by the Secretary of State for Education and Employment, Greenwich, 15 February.

Brown, R. (2003) New Labour and higher education: dilemmas and paradoxes, *Higher Education Quarterly,* 57(3), 239–248.

Brown, R. (2005) Education, education, education—but will government policies produce an 'excellent higher education system'? *Higher Education Review,* 38(1), 3–31.

Brown, R. (2006) Higher Education and the market: protecting quality and diversity in a market-driven system, *Higher Education Review,* 39(1), 3–16.

Dearing, R. (2007) Afterword, in: D. Watson & M. Amoah (Eds) *The Dearing Report ten years on* (London, Institute of Education, University of London).

DfES (Department for Education and Skills) (2003a) *The future of Higher Education* Government White Paper (London, The Stationery Office).

DfES (Department for Education and Skills) (2003b) *Widening participation in Higher Education* (London, The Stationery Office).

Gallacher, J. (2006) Widening access or differentiation and stratification in higher education in Scotland, *Higher Education Quarterly,* 60(4), 349–369.

Jenkins, S. (2007) *Thatcher and her sons: a revolution in three Acts* (London, Allen & Lane).

Lawton, D. (2005) *Education and Labour Party ideologies 1900–2001 and beyond* (Abingdon, RoutledgeFalmer).

Lee, A. & Boud, D. (2009) Framing doctoral education as practice, in: D. Boud & A. Lee (Eds) *Changing practices of doctoral education* (London, Routledge).

Morley, L. & Aynsley, S. (2007) Employees, quality and standards in higher education: shared values and vocabularies or elitism and inequalities? *Higher Education Quarterly,* 61(3), 229–249.

Naidoo, R. (2003) Repositioning higher education as a global commodity: opportunities and challenges for future of sociology of education work, *British Journal of Sociology of Education,* 24(3), 249–259.

Naidoo, R. & Jamieson, I. (2005) Empowering participants or corroding learning? Towards a research agenda on the impact of student consumerism in Higher Education, *Journal of Education Policy,* 20(3), 267–281.

NCIHE (National Committee of Inquiry into Higher Education) (1997) *Higher Education in the learning society* (the Dearing Report) (London, HMSO).

O'Leary, J. (2007) Higher Education, in: A. Seldon (Ed.) *Blair's Britain 1997–2007* (Cambridge, Cambridge University Press).

Paterson, L. (2003) The three educational ideologies of the British Labour Party, 1997–2001, *Oxford Review of Education,* 29(2), 165–186.

Power, S. & Whitty, G. (1999) New Labour's education policy: first, second or third way? *Journal of Education Policy,* 14, 535–546.

Rees, G. & Taylor, C. (2006) Devolution and the restructuring of participation in HE in Wales, *Higher Education Quarterly,* 60(4), 370–391.

Scott, P. (1995) *The meanings of mass higher education* (Buckingham, SRHE and Open University Press).

Shattock, M. (2008) The change from private to public governance of Higher Education: its consequences for HE policy-making 1980–2006, *Higher Education Quarterly,* 62(3), 181–203.

Tight, M. (2006) Institutional diversity in English Higher Education, *Higher Educational Review,* 39(2), 3–24.

Tomlinson, S. (2001) *Education in a post-welfare society* (Buckingham, Open University Press).

Watson, D. (2007) *Whatever happened to the Dearing report? UK Higher Education 1997–2007* (London, Institute of Education, University of London).

Watts, M. & Bridges, D. (2006) The value of non-participation in Higher Education, *Journal of Education Policy*, 21(3), 267–290.

Whitty, G. (2002) *Making sense of education policy* (London, Paul Chapman).

Wolf, A. (2002) *Does education matter? Myths about education and economic growth* (London, Penguin).

New Labour, education and Wales: the devolution decade

David Reynolds

Introduction

The Government of Wales Act in 1998 devolved to the National Assembly for Wales a wide range of powers that had formerly been exercised by the United Kingdom (UK) government. Essentially, a small Civil Service in Wales had implemented and, in some cases, adapted policies that were jointly 'England and Wales' in orientation, and in the case of cultural issues to do with the Welsh language's position in society and in education there was additionally evidence of widespread policy innovation.

However, the devolution of power to spend the 'block grant' (the combined expenditures of different Ministries on Wales before devolution) plus powers to construct its own policies and priorities concerning the spending of that money was a landmark in the history of Wales, and to a lesser extent also of Scotland and Northern Ireland (Scotland had been exercising many of these powers historically in any case, and Northern Ireland had fewer powers devolved to exercise).

It was probably never intended that there would be a resulting 'policy laboratory' in which the different nations of the UK attempted radically different solutions to the major issues of the day—it seems likely that devolution was designed to improve *delivery* of services in accordance with locally defined needs, rather than being designed to generate different *policies* themselves. Nevertheless, in Wales in many areas—and in the area of education and training in particular—the three Welsh Assembly Governments (WAGs) from 1999/2003, 2003/2007, and 2007 to date have generated in public services generally, and in education in particular, a 'Welsh Alternative' to those provided in England, and to policies now seen as axiomatic internationally. That policy opportunity to innovate has now been furthered by the Government of Wales Act which confers the power to generate primary legislation, from 2006.

Describing the Welsh way, the factors which generated it, analysing its possible successes and failures and assessing the lessons of it for the UK and International educational policies are the subjects of this paper.

The New Labour Context

In England, New Labour pursued a range of policies concerned with public sector reform which, although their content and tone changed and developed over time, amounted to a consistent philosophy of how government should provide state welfare. Expenditure was increased, both recurrent and capital, to improve numbers of professionals in public services and to make up for historic underfunding. The volume of provider organisations was increased, with the addition of increased numbers of private sector companies and more recent enhanced use of 'third sector' voluntary and charitable organisations.

The public sector was tied to 'performance targets' and performance data on its operation at individual locations like schools and hospitals was placed in the public domain to aid 'consumer choice'. The variety of types of provision was also expanded to provide objects for that choice to root. In more recent years, these attempts have been supplemented by Gerschon (2004) based attempts to cut public sector numbers and expenditure.

The 'consumerist' orientation of policies was complemented, though, by a considerable volume of governmental intervention in the delivery of welfare, through direct provision of professional knowledge and professional training, thus being simultaneously concerned with 'pressure and support'.

In Wales, there has been a concern to show 'clear red water' between English and Welsh policies on state welfare. The left wing political history of Wales and the use of government to ensure enhanced social justice for Welsh citizens created a climate of greater trust in provider determined solutions, the 'producerism' that sits in contrast to English 'consumerism'. One of the Welsh First Minister's advisers, Drakeford (2006), characterised the Welsh approach as based upon social justice, universalism, trust of providers, and equality of outcomes. The Welsh First Minister himself (Morgan, 2002) argued that 'Approaches which prioritise choice over equality of outcome rest, in the end, upon a market approach to public services, in which individual economic actors pursue their own best interests with little regard for wider considerations'. The Welsh paradigm is, conventionally, that the State provides.

Given these ideological commitments, it is not surprising that the English regime of Public Sector Targets is less entrenched in Wales, that use of the Public Finance Initiative (PFI) is less, that Public/Private Partnerships are largely neglected, that public sector savings targets are lower and later in operation, and that there has been an absence of some of the harsh rhetoric with which New Labour has addressed government in England.

By contrast, the Welsh approach to public sector reform has been to argue for improved efficiency through 'collaborative working' between service providers as outlined in the documents *Making The Connections* (WAG, 2004, 2005) and the 'citizenship' model (Beecham, 2006), whereby the emphasis is to be upon improving service delivery through participation, collaboration and change in culture, capacity and processes.

Educational policy paradigms in England and Wales

In England, using the knowledge bases provided by the school effectiveness and school improvement communities that were adopted by New Labour's principal education adviser Michael Barber (1996) a coherent package of educational reform was set out that was concerned with both pressure and support:

- There was a belief in the 'human capital' thesis and a commitment to using the educational system to generate increased student educational outcomes, seen as necessary to enable the United Kingdom to compete in an increasingly globalised economy (see Robinson, 1997 for a critique);
- There was a belief that 'standards' not 'structures' mattered more, indicating that debates about selective or comprehensive organisational patterns were to be replaced by an enhanced focus on the more important within-school drivers of educational achievement like teaching methods when New Labour became a government;
- There was, indeed, a pervasive view that the teaching profession was itself responsible for some of the problems with achieving higher standards, since it was seen as insular, reluctant to learn lessons from public and private provision outside education and also unwilling to recognise and benchmark against its own best people (for further discussion on these themes see Reynolds, 2002a, 2003, 2006).

Whilst New Labour believed that social class and social and economic disadvantage were key factors in holding back the achievement outcomes of certain groups of children, the emphasis of the party was upon the difference that schools made and how the educational system on its own could achieve much, if reformed. Indeed, the New Labour project, from the arrival of David Blunkett as Education Shadow Spokesperson in 1995, was notably critical towards schools and teachers, even endorsing some of the attacks made on producers by Chris Woodhead, the Chief Inspector of English schools (Blunkett, 2006).

Nevertheless, there was an optimism to English policy in which educational problems were seen not as being due to the absence of knowledge about how to educate children effectively (validity issues) but as due to the inability of all schools to do as the best schools did (reliability issues). Research that showed considerable variation between schools (Reynolds, 1995; Sammons *et al.*, 1997; Teddlie & Reynolds, 2002) was therefore enthusiastically embraced.

Whilst there was a clear blueprint for English education when Labour became a government in 1997, for schools in Wales no comparable thinking to inform policy development had been done. Whilst in Scotland the presence of devolved powers in all areas of education (including Pay and Conditions, training and indeed professional standards) had been aided by a fertile growth in think-tanks, policy institutes and pressure groups, in Wales only one such organisation existed at the time of the mid-1990s—The Institute for Welsh Affairs (although an organisation entitled the Bevan Foundation now exists additionally).

Wales had exercised devolved powers in education since the establishment of the Education Department of the Welsh Office in the 1960s, and there was a separate Welsh curriculum and assessment organisation and a separate curriculum that incorporated Welsh as a compulsory subject in the 'core' requirements of the Welsh national curriculum as it emerged in the 1990s. There had also been distinctively Welsh approaches to education and training in the mid to late 1990s that indeed became an example for subsequent English approaches (Rees, 2002).

But much of the effort—emotional and practical—of the embryonic Welsh educational state had been focused on improving the status of the Welsh language, not on the broader issues of enhanced effectiveness and improvement in student outcomes that influenced the English policy paradigm from 1997. Also, within Wales there was little of the micro-level work into 'effective' schools that was to become so influential in England. High quality work existed in a wide range of areas such as assessment (e.g. Daugherty, 1995) and the history of education (e.g. Evans, 1990; Jones, 1997). There was additionally high quality material on the effects of parental choice on social inequalities (e.g. Gorard, 1997; Gorard & Fitz, 2000a, 2000b) and on adult/lifelong education (e.g. Rees *et al.*, 1997; Gorard *et al.*, 1998).

But there was in Wales considerable hostility to the school effectiveness knowledge base that was involved and implicated in English educational policymaking, that involved trenchant critiques of some of the studies (e.g. Gorard, 1998 a, b, c) and a clear dislike of the paradigm. Gorard (2002, p. 82) noted that 'school effectiveness has become a kind of cult … the movement is becoming more and more part of the official discourse, mixed with economic vocabulary about targets for lifelong learning and market driven performance indicators'.

In the absence, then, of any clear school and classroom level policy levers in Wales equivalent to those provided by the effectiveness literature in England, and with hostility to the English policies, the tenure of the first two Education Ministers of the Assembly (Tom Middlehurst and Rosemary Butler) was marked by a principle of not doing what England did, since England was seen as embracing prescription of practice. Thus, the English Literacy and Numeracy Strategies that involved a comprehensive series of programmes that were delivered to all primary school teachers from 1998 had no Welsh parallel, other than some brief recapitulation of what was effective practice in hard copy and video format, but produced in limited numbers and available only 'on request', not distributed to all. The National College for School Leadership likewise, which was intended to resource Heads and Senior Managers with notions of what was 'effective leadership', was set up in 2001 with no Welsh parallel.

For the schools sector these attempts have been called 'new producerism' (Reynolds, 2006), in that they rejected the New Labour belief that the methods of ensuring that quality improved was through changing the outside contingencies within which the education system was situated, through publication of information on quality/results, and through parental choice and an enhanced variety of schools from which parents could choose. This English consumerism was of course likely to be much less appropriate in Wales, since there were long traditions of parents choosing their local community primary and/or secondary schools, since there was no competitive independent sector that parents could opt into, and since many areas of Wales, such as the rural and small town communities, may have had only one school within reasonable travelling distance from home in any case, thereby reducing effective choice.

But the 'new producerism' of Wales extended beyond a simple rejection of the English, and indeed international, trend to 'consumerism'. It believed that working 'with', rather than 'on' or 'to', educational professionals was likely to be more effective than the emphasis in the consumerist paradigm about accountability of them. Discussion on education in Wales, as in Scotland, was therefore notably less critical of the professionals than in England—they were to be trusted, to be listened to and to be respected rather than criticised and 'shamed' as in some English educational policy discourse. Indeed, the historic closeness between the teaching unions and the Welsh Labour Party, and the emphasis within the Welsh Assembly Government on a 'team Wales' approach, were further reinforcers of the consensual approach to education policy that evolved during Jane Davidson's tenure as Education Minister, in which policy moved from being reactive (not doing what England did) to proactive (outlining new policy means) from 2001.

There was also in Wales a commitment to the community-based comprehensive school, and a refusal to differentiate the secondary school system into the variety of 'types' of school such as Academies and varieties of Specialist Schools or Trusts as in the English consumerist model. Additionally, whilst Wales had never published the achievement test data (or SATs) on its individual primary schools as had England, the results of secondary schools that were published in both England and Wales in the form of national 'league tables' were, in Wales from 2003, only published by individual local authorities about their own schools rather than in a national 'league table'.

The path that was being followed in Wales did not simply reflect a rejection of the New Labour commitment to the 'market' based solutions of England, which had found in the 'efficiency, effectiveness and improvement' paradigms intellectual justification and detailed content from which policy could be derived. Partly, it also reflected an historical commitment in Wales to the use of the education system to *transform* society, rather than maintain the existing relations of production, and to achieve social justice for different societal groups, both of which were reflected in the phrase 'clear red water' and the belief in co-operation and universalism that we noted earlier. Naturally, Wales has also had much less involvement of private sector provision.

The differences between England and Wales also extended to the delivery mechanisms for educational provision, since English New Labour evidenced a marked hostility to local government that had no Welsh parallel. In England, a robust regime of 'capping' local authorities that spent over certain levels was combined with a policy that forced local authorities to 'devolve' a high proportion of their educational budgets to individual secondary schools, with local authorities holding back progressively less of the total received from central government. This was combined from the mid-2000s with direct payments to schools from central government in England.

Whereas in England only approximately 5% of educational expenditure was retained to cover local authority services by 2007, in Wales the situation was very different. In the early 2000s, 17% of total education revenue grant was held back by local councils, a figure that *rose* over time to reach 24.2% by the 2006/7 financial year. Additionally, there were no direct payments at all to individual schools in Wales (National Assembly for Wales, 2006). Of course, some of the differences between the two countries in the financial arrangements of local authorities are likely to be more apparent than real, since a proportion of the delegated budget to schools is used by the schools of many English authorities to simply 'buy back' the local authority services they are provided with.

But the different relationship between schools and their local authorities in Wales and in England clearly reflects a different settlement at national policy making level too. It has been argued (Osmond, 1978) that in Wales historically society has been seen as operating on three levels—that of the individual, the local community and the nation—whereas in England the much discussed 'decline' of communities and the rapid accretion of central government powers means that the most influential levels (in terms of determinants of society) are only the two of the individual and the nation (for further speculations on this theme see Reynolds & Pritchard Jones, 1999; Reynolds, 2002b, 2003).

The results of the salience of Welsh local authorities in the lives of schools—without English parallel—has been widely seen as negative by teacher unions and professional associations (e.g. Secondary Heads Association Cymru, 2005). It is argued that the budget which a headteacher in England receives for an average size secondary school of 900 pupils will be perhaps £500,000 more in England, and that this and local authority holdback in Wales reduces the morale of heads in Wales. In England this has been improved by giving heads greater budgetary control, the enhanced ability to vire across expenditure areas and the capacity to replace local authority services with private providers should they so want, it is argued.

Reflecting the 'new producerist' paradigm described above, Wales proceeded with different initiatives on, for example:

- The abolition of externally based assessment of pupils in Key Stages One, Two and Three, recommended by the Daugherty Committee and much welcomed by 'producer' interests;
- The pattern of funding of student support for students in FE and HE, with the Assembly Learning Grant available to those in both sectors since 2002, unlike in England;
- The pattern of student support in HE from 2007, involving partial remission of the 'top up' fees for Welsh domiciled students;
- The development and piloting of the Welsh Baccalaureate, a 'Core' added to existing 'A' levels designed to broaden the sixth-form curriculum;
- The development of the framework of age 14–19 Learning Pathways within which individuals chose from a series of offers containing both a learning Core (a set of experiences in common) and a variety of support involving Learning Coaches, personal support and specialist careers advice.

It would be wrong to emphasise the differences between Labour policies in England and in Wales without describing also the similarities. The reduction of class sizes in the primary age phase below a size of 30 was pursued in both societies. Improvement in the physical state of the buildings of schools and colleges was a goal in both societies, although the English level of capital spend has been running at approximately three times the Welsh figure per head of population.

Enhanced early years provision, in Wales as in England, involved the growth of integrated children's services, Flying Start (similar to the English 'Sure Start') and most recently the development in Wales of the Foundation Phase for children aged 3–7, in which a curriculum focused upon learning basic social competencies through structured play and other activities will be implemented over the four years from Autumn 2008.

Likewise, both societies have shown concern with school non-attendance, with the NEETs (those Not in Employment, Education or Training), and with personalisation of the secondary school offer to reflect the increasingly diverse needs of the student population. Issues to do with the 'gender gap' between girls and the lower performing boys have also been addressed in both societies. Both societies have reformed their inspection arrangements for schools, with the Welsh Inspectorate ESTYN moving towards a framework similar to that of the English Ofsted (Office for Standards in Education) in its enhanced focus on assessing school capacity to self-review and self-improve.

It is also important to note that there were also elements within Welsh policies that did not fit any simple 'new producerist' label. The introduction of a Children's Commissioner, the statutory commitment to Children's and Young People's Partnerships and the introduction of School Councils from Autumn 2006 all increased the rights of the child 'consumer'. Post-16, in areas of Wales where there was no tertiary provision, there was a consumer choice between schools and colleges, and there was competition between colleges and training providers for work-based learning (further details of Welsh policies can be found in Welsh Assembly Government, 2001, 2006).

Nevertheless, in their tone, content and organisation, the policies pursued in Wales have been very different from those of England. Whilst English educational policies in recent years have been more concerned to 'support' schools than to 'pressure' them, and whilst the English system has been more concerned to develop 'laterality' rather than its historic 'verticality' of late, making it in orientation more like the Welsh system, it is clear that two very different paradigms about the nature of the school/society/state relationship are being explored here in the two societies.

The effects of the Welsh alternative

Assessing the effects of educational policies pursued in different countries—even two similar societies—is notoriously difficult, given the wide variety of influences—economic, social, political and cultural—that may be implicated. The data available are customarily only on a very limited range of outcomes, such as participation rates, attendance rates and levels of academic achievement measured by examinations, and do not provide measures of broader individual or collective social attributes such as self confidence, locus of control and other 'social' or 'affective' outcomes that are regarded as increasingly important within modern societies.

Also, data even of the limited kind noted above are not 'value added' when analysed by nation, in the way that is now axiomatic when they are examined by school. In country comparative work, there are no studies that look at the 'value added' growth and development of student populations over time, with the exception of the small scale *World Class Schools* study (Reynolds *et al.*, 2002).

However, examination of the data we do possess shows a remarkable consistency in that Welsh performance relative to England has been declining. On simple measures such as the percentage of students achieving at least 5 A* to C GCSE passes, a gap of 0.2% in favour of England in 2000/2001 has become one of 8% by 2006/2007 (Reynolds, 2006; ESTYN, 2008). The proportion of students with no measured examination achievements at GCSE is higher in Wales than in England and has fallen less quickly (Reynolds, 2006). Interestingly, these kinds of comparisons over time largely 'control out' the influence of socioeconomic factors which are, of course, relatively unchanged over time.

The PISA 2006 studies (OECD, 2007) also give cause for concern about the relative success of Welsh policies. Out of the four home nations of the United Kingdom (England, Northern Ireland, Scotland and Wales), Wales was below the other three countries in all three subjects tested of mathematics, science and reading. Although it is possible that broader social and economic influences are responsible for these results and that poor Welsh performance reflects these non-educational factors, the countries of Scotland and Northern Ireland both have *higher* levels of social deprivation than Wales in terms of unemployment, poor housing and the proportion of their population of low social class, predisposing *them* to be the poorer performers. Additionally, Northern Ireland retains an almost exclusively selective secondary education system, with its secondary modern schools predisposing it to likely poor performance in addition to its deprivation levels. The differences between nations are small, it must be noted, but are consistent.

However, since Welsh performance is relatively better in science than in the other two subject areas, and since science is relatively more school/teacher dependant (since most families do not expose their children to science at home in the way they do for reading and mathematics), blanket judgements about the relative ineffectiveness of the Welsh system are unwise (see Teddlie & Reynolds, 2002, for evidence on subject differences in school effects).

It is also important to note that historic attempts to argue that the education system of Wales was more 'ineffective' than that of England (Reynolds, 1990) have been rightly criticised as not comparing like with like, which in this case should have involved comparing Wales with English regions of similar socio-economic composition like the North East. If this is done, then Wales performs similarly (Gorard, 2002).

However, Wales's *lower* levels of deprivation than Scotland and Northern Ireland, and its *poorer* performance, are suggestive here. Additionally, the Welsh system performs at a level equivalent to England at Key Stages One and Two, but much more poorly at Key Stage Three and poorly at Key Stage Four. Socio-economic explanations cannot explain these differences at different ages, suggesting again some kind of systemic explanation (Reynolds, 2008).

Interestingly, the poor overall Welsh PISA performance is particularly due to underperformance at the higher achievement levels, which suggests that Welsh schools may have responded to much historic criticism that they have been concerned with the able by turning their attention subsequently, disproportionately, to the 'floor', a change that may have been encouraged by the WAG focus on the Basic Skills Agenda. Additionally, it is possible that the English emphasis upon the education of the able through its Gifted and Talented activities may have had an effect, although this would not explain the better Scottish performance with high achievers of course.

There are some hints in the science survey that material differences in schools in Wales may be a part of the explanation. Headteachers were asked about the adequacy and availability of resources such as 'IT' and 'instructional materials' like books and published schemes of work. Welsh Headteachers were more likely to report inadequate provision than the average across-the-world figures, a surprising finding since a great many of the PISA participating countries were low spending, developing societies like Croatia and Azerbaijan. If these countries were to be stripped out, then Welsh material performance would be probably even more inadequate than the remaining 'developed society' sample.

A further possible explanation for poor Welsh performance relative to England is the tendency for Wales to fall behind England as expenditure on education in both countries has increased over time. By the 2006/7 academic year, expenditure per student was 7.7% higher in England than in Wales, by comparison with only a 1% difference in 2000/1. Given the similarity in class sizes, teacher salaries and pupil–teacher ratios in the two countries, it is possible that the Welsh system has little 'discretionary' expenditure on non-core activities left after the cores are taken care of (further speculations are in National Assembly for Wales, 2006).

A further possibility for poor Welsh results is that Wales has a poor delivery mechanism in its educational authorities. They have a high salience because of high 'hold-back' and their number—22 local authorities for a nation of 3.5 million—may not provide an ideal setting for educational improvement. They are too big to be able to relate easily to a local 'patch' and too small in most cases to be capable of high level strategic thinking. Their variability is notable, with a range of £1,400 in the amount spent per student between the highest and lowest spending authorities. The ESTYN Annual Report also notes that the quality of local authorities is 'patchy', with one third said to be 'poor' and two thirds 'unlikely to improve' (ESTYN, 2008)—which are quite extraordinary assessments. The extent to which the new School Effectiveness Framework will reduce this variation is unclear (Welsh Assembly Government, 2008).

Overall, it is difficult to find convincing evidence that the distinctively Welsh 'new producerism', combined with a conventional commitment to social justice is delivering, although the extent to which this reflects a 'quality of policy' dimension or the simple 'quantity' of resource allocated to education in Wales or the delivery mechanism is unclear. The extent to which the system has been successful in 'equity' areas rather than 'excellence' is, of course, unknown.

Conclusions

It is difficult not to appreciate the scale of the enterprise—emotional, organisational and intellectual—required to develop an innovative, extensive and coherent set of policies on education in Wales post devolution. It was precisely the space offered to Wales to develop its own policies by the New Labour constitutional settlement that made this possible. Both the policies, and the space that made them possible, will rightly be seen as a major legacy, together with the comparable developments in education and other public sector areas in Scotland and Northern Ireland.

But it is important also to acknowledge that what can be seen as a producerist ideology may not have been entirely effective in improving educational outcomes, although whether this is due to the policies themselves, their implementation, their resource base, or to a combination of factors, is unclear. What might be the lessons of the attempt, for Wales and for educational policies more generally?

First, education in Wales had to compete for attention against the problems of administrative reorganisation, nation building and the continued commitment to the development of the Welsh language and culture, all of which meant that it may have been difficult to prioritise educational concerns in the way that the somewhat obsessional commitment to 'Education, Education, Education' influenced New Labour in England. Successful educational change necessitates prioritising of education that may not have happened adequately in Wales.

Second, and linked with the first point, it is somewhat ironic that Wales has not delivered financial resources to education to the degree that England has, ironic given the more 'socialistic' orientation, or rhetoric at least, of Welsh society. Between 2000/2001 and 2004/2005 the proportion of WAG spending devoted to education and training actually fell (from 16% to 15%) with economic development increasing from

3% to 13% (some of this was due to the need to 'match fund' the Objective One EEC Structural Fund programme grants, but not all). In terms of percentage change over time, education and training expenditure increased by only 43.2%, compared with 151% for economic development, 46% for transport, 156% for the environment, 49.8% for health, 63% for culture and 54% for public expenditure in Wales generally (see Institute for Welsh Affairs, 2006, for more details). Successful educational change requires adequate resourcing, which may not have happened in Wales.

Third, little attempt was made to build the capacity of the Welsh system to innovate and change. Whether or not the resourcing of the profession (1999–2003) with knowledge about 'good practice' or the more lateral notions of schools learning from other schools (2003–2008) was the chosen method, England attempted to build the 'capacity' that is now regarded as axiomatic in literatures about transformative change internationally (Reynolds, 2002, 2005, 2007). It is interesting that the School Effectiveness Framework will provide knowledge to all schools in Wales over the next four years, and was informed by four international experts from the effectiveness/improvement paradigm associated with English New Labour. The Foundation Phase will also involve extensive training and capacity building. It should also be noted that capacity within the Higher Education system to monitor, evaluate and develop new educational policies may also have been absent in Wales (Furlong & White, 2001). Successful educational change requires capacity building at all levels, which may not have been present in Wales.

Overall, it is difficult to avoid the conclusion that the legacy of devolution to Wales, and the policies that were followed after it, validate much of what can be called the New Labour educational paradigm of England. England spent more, prioritised more heavily and attended to the building of capacity more than Wales. But whether it was the Welsh delivery mechanisms that were ineffective, rather than the policies, remains unclear. Also, it may be that Welsh policies—like the Foundation Phase—may have a longer term effect. It would be ironic, though, and clearly unanticipated, if the legacy of Welsh devolution was to validate different sets of policies than those attempted in Wales.

References

Barber, M. (1996) *The learning game—arguments for an education revolution* (London, Victor Gallancz).

Beecham, J. (2006) *Beyond boundaries: citizen centred local services for Wales* (Cardiff, WAG).
Blunkett, D. (2006) *The Blunkett tapes: my life in the bear pit* (London, Bloomsbury).
Daugherty, R. (1995) *National Curriculum assessment: a review of policy 1987–1994* (Lewes, Falmer Press).
Drakeford, M. (2006) Progressive universalism, *Agenda, The Journal of the Institute for Welsh Affairs,* Winter.
ESTYN (2008) *The annual report of Her Majesty's Chief Inspector of Education and Training in Wales,* 2006/7 (Cardiff, ESTYN).
Evans, G. (Ed.) (1990) *Perspectives on a century of secondary education in Wales* (Aberystwyth, Centre for Educational Studies).
Furlong, J. & White, P. (2001) *Educational research capacity in Wales* (Cardiff, Cardiff University School of Social Sciences).
Gerschon, P. (2004) *Independent review of public sector efficiency: releasing resources to the front line* (London, HM Government).
Gorard, S. (1997) *School choice in an established market* (Aldershot, Ashgate).
Gorard, S. (1998a) In defence of local comprehensive schools in South Wales, *Forum,* 40(2), 58–59.
Gorard, S. (1998b) Four errors and a conspiracy? The effectiveness of schools in Wales, *Oxford Review of Education,* 24(4), 459–472.
Gorard, S. (1998c) Schooled to fail? Revisiting the Welsh school effect, *Journal of Education Policy,* 13(1), 115–124.
Gorard, S. (2002) *Education and social justice* (Cardiff, University of Wales Press).
Gorard, S. & Fitz, J. (2000a) Investigating the determinants of segregation between schools, *Research Papers in Education,* 15(2), 115–132.
Gorard, S. & Fitz, J. (2000b) Do markets lead to satisfaction? The experience of schools in England and Wales, *Educational Policy,* 14(3), 405–428.
Gorard, S., Rees, G., Fevre, R. & Furlong, J. (1998) Learning trajectories: travelling towards a learning society, *International Journal of Lifelong Education,* 17(6), 400–410.
Institute for Welsh Affairs (2006) *Time to deliver* (Cardiff, IWA).
Jones, G. E. (1997) *The education of a nation* (Cardiff, University of Wales Press).
Morgan, R. (2002) *Third anniversary lecture* (Swansea, National Centre for Public Policy).
National Assembly for Wales (2006) *Committee on school funding—report on school funding arrangements in Wales* (Cardiff, National Assembly for Wales).
OECD (Organisation for Economic Cooperation and Development) (2007) *Programme for International Student Assessment (PISA)* (OECD, Paris).
Osmond, J. (1978) *Creative conflict: the politics of Welsh devolution* (Llandysul, Gomer Press).
Rees, G. (2002) Devolution and the restructuring of post-16 education and training in the UK, in: J. Adams & P. Robinson (2002) *Devolution in practice: public policy differences within the UK* (London, IPPR).
Rees, G., Fevre, R., Furlong, J. & Gorard, S. (1997) History, place and the learning society: towards a society of lifelong learning, *Journal of Education Policy,* 12(6), 485–497.
Reynolds, D. (1990) The great Welsh education debate, *History of Education,* 19(3), 251–257.
Reynolds, D. (1995) The effective school: an inaugural lecture, *Evaluation and Research in Education,* 9(2), 57–73.
Reynolds, D. (2002a) School effectiveness, school improvement and contemporary educational policies, in: J. Demaine (Ed.) *Contemporary educational policy and politics* (2nd edn.) (London, Macmillan), 65–81.
Reynolds, D. (2002b) Developing differently: educational policy in England, Wales, Scotland and Northern Ireland, in J. Adams & P. Robinson (Eds) *Devolution in practice: public policy differences within the UK* (London, ESRC/IPPR).
Reynolds, D. (2003) Education: building on difference, in: J. Osmond (Ed.) *Second term challenge: can the Welsh Assembly hold its course?* (Cardiff, The Institute for Welsh Affairs).

Reynolds, D. (2005) How can recent research in school effectiveness, teacher effectiveness and school improvement inform our thinking about educational policies? in: D. Hopkins, D. Reynolds & J. Gray (Eds) *School improvement: lessons from research* (London, Department for Education and Skills).

Reynolds, D. (2006) Education, in: The Institute for Welsh Affairs, *Time to deliver: the third term and beyond* (Cardiff, The Institute for Welsh Affairs).

Reynolds, D. (2007) School effectiveness and school improvement: links with the international accountability and standards agenda, in: T. Townsend (Ed.) *The international handbook of school effectiveness and school improvement* (Dordrecht: Springer), 471–484.

Reynolds, D. (2008) It boils down to money, *Times Educational Supplement Cymru,* 25 July, p. 21.

Reynolds, D. & Pritchard Jones, E. (1999) Education, in: J. Osmond (Ed.) *The National Assembly agenda* (Llandysul, Gomer Press).

Reynolds, D., Creemers, B. P. M., Stringfield, S., Teddlie, C. & Schaffer, G. (2002) *World class schools: international perspectives on school effectiveness* (London, Routledge).

Robinson, P. (1997) *Literacy, numeracy and economic performance* (London, Centre for Economic Performance, London School of Economics).

Sammons, P., Mortimore, P. & Thomas, S. (1997) *Forging limits: effective schools and effective departments* (London, Paul Chapman).

Secondary Heads Association Cymru (2005) *The funding of secondary schools in Wales* (Leicester, SHA).

Teddlie, C. & Reynolds, D. (2002) *The international handbook of school effectiveness research* (London, RoutledgeFalmer).

Welsh Assembly Government (2001) *The learning country* (Cardiff, WAG).

Welsh Assembly Government (2004) *Making the connections: visions for public services* (Cardiff, WAG).

Welsh Assembly Government (2005) *Delivering the connections: from vision to action* (Cardiff, WAG).

Welsh Assembly Government (2006) *The learning country—vision into action* (Cardiff, WAG).

Welsh Assembly Government (2008) *School effectiveness framework* (Cardiff, WAG).

Evaluating 'Blair's Educational Legacy?': some comments on the special issue of *Oxford Review of Education*

Geoff Whitty

Introduction

This paper arose from the response I gave at a keynote symposium at the British Educational Research Association (BERA) annual conference in Edinburgh in September 2008. The five papers I was commenting on—by Richard Hatcher, Neil Selwyn, David Gillborn, Ingrid Lunt and David Reynolds—were among the papers now included in the special issue of the *Oxford Review of Education* published in

December 2008 (ORE, 2008). In that publication, they were accompanied by additional papers from Diane Reay, Pam Sammons, Richard Pring, Geoffrey Walford and John Furlong. The majority of the contributors work in the sociology of education, which is also my own specialism. Not surprisingly, there is a strong emphasis in many of the papers, and in this response, on the impact or otherwise of New Labour policies on social inequalities.

The symposium and the publication aim to give 'an evaluation of what has been accomplished and what might be the longer-term legacy' of the Blair years for education (p. 1, this volume). As the convenor of the symposium and editor of the special issue, Geoffrey Walford, has recognised, the collection of papers does not provide a 'comprehensive' assessment of the Blair legacy in education (p. 1). Furthermore, each of the papers deals with a specific aspect of the legacy of the Blair government. This means there is not much of a sense in the volume of the overall achievements of New Labour to date. Most of the papers are particularly focused on secondary education and there are also some areas, notably the so-called 'children's agenda' and 'lifelong learning', that are relatively neglected. The absence of a sustained discussion of early years provision in this collection is particularly regrettable, not least because it is usually considered one of New Labour's greatest achievements. It is also the one part of New Labour education policy that regularly receives plaudits from the academic left and the one that is most clearly grounded in evidence produced by educational researchers (see Siraj-Blatchford *et al.*, 2008).

The individual contributions

Pam Sammons' discussion of New Labour approaches to school improvement in England (pp. 14–27) is one of the more balanced papers in the collection. She highlights the achievements of New Labour in raising attainment overall, but is concerned about the ever-changing definitions of success and failure and the relative lack of improvement for the most disadvantaged pupils. Despite rising attainment levels and a widening of participation, there has therefore been little narrowing of long-standing and sizeable attainment gaps. As a result, Blair's education policies have so far had only modest success in combating social exclusion, though she notes that 'investment in early years may yet show longer term benefits' (p. 25). She concludes that, despite improvements over the last decade and New Labour's 'zero tolerance' of failure, the extent to which schools can overcome the effects of social disadvantage remains limited (p. 25).

Diane Reay offers an almost exclusively negative assessment of the New Labour legacy in her discussion of Tony Blair's promotion of parental choice and its role in sustaining middle-class hegemony (pp. 2–13). She argues that, while Blair understood the middle-class psyche very well, he was much less well informed about working-class cultures and experiences (p. 9). She claims that he has left 'a trail of failed policies that, rather than reducing inequality, have sedimented and augmented middle-class advantage in the educational field, a sad record for any political leader but a travesty for a Labour one' (p. 10). Ultimately Blair's legacy is seen as retaining and expanding neo-liberal education polices, which have exacerbated inequality. Indeed, she identifies continuity between Conservative and Labour policies on the role of parents, both before and after the Blair era. She concludes that 'what is clear is that Blair and his inheritors across the political spectrum offer no radical solutions to educational inequality, in fact no solutions at all' (p. 10). Yet nor does Reay herself really suggest what alternatives might be pursued if, as she hopes, the current agenda is abandoned.

Geoffrey Walford's contribution on the role of faith-based schools in England after ten years of Tony Blair (pp. 52–62) discusses one particular aspect of the school choice and school autonomy agenda that seems to have gained prominence as a result of Blair's personal beliefs. What Walford sees as 'a slightly more diverse and more multi-faith system of schools in the state-maintained sector' (p. 60) is reflected not only in the encouragement of more faith-based voluntary schools but also in the proportion of Academies with faith-based sponsors. At the same time as presenting existing (mainly Christian denominational) faith schools as particularly effective, New Labour has also embraced schools of other faiths. However, Walford regards that as an inevitable product of an increasingly multi-faith society rather than a unique feature of New Labour policy. As he puts it, 'it is difficult to see how any other government could have not agreed to funding Muslim, Sikh, Hindu and other minority faith schools, given that various types of Christian and Jewish schools had this advantage' (p. 60). He notes that the changes since Blair left office, such as local authorities now being involved in decisions about the establishment of Academies, may temper Blair's legacy for faith schools, but overall 'Blair may have simply delayed the inevitable debate that is needed about the role of faith-based schools in a modern society' (p. 61).

Richard Hatcher's paper, 'Academies and diplomas: two strategies for shaping the future workforce' (pp. 28–39), provides a more sustained discussion of the Academies policy in general along with a critique of the introduction of Diplomas. The link is that both policies are, in their different ways, business-related. He sees both as part of a second phase of New Labour education policy after an initial one focused on the 'standards agenda', which he regards as having failed far more comprehensively than Sammons suggests. He believes that the production of 'human capital' was the master narrative of policy under Blair, building on an emphasis on the economic function of education that goes back to the Callaghan government in 1976 (p. 28). Following subsequent Conservative policies of marketisation and state regulation, the Blair government is seen by Hatcher as having overseen an unprecedented degree of privatisation of education provision on a for-profit basis. Yet, he asserts that 'Blair has bequeathed to his successors two major reforms in the school system which seem unlikely to resolve the fundamental problem of supplying the workforce it is claimed that capital requires and thereby providing the basis for a durable policy settlement' (p. 36). Unlike most of the contributors, Hatcher does consider the future of the policies and contemplates a possible alternative, whereby the neo-liberal agenda is rejected.

Richard Pring provides a more balanced assessment of policies for the 14–19 age group and commends many aspects of New Labour's wider education polices, such as Every Child Matters, especially in their conception (pp. 40–51). He notes that there has been a shift in emphasis to encouraging education and training for 14–19 year olds of all backgrounds and describes efforts to integrate services, and the establishment of partnerships to achieve this, as being 'in many ways' laudable (p. 50). However, problems such as the academic/vocational divide are economically and socially deep rooted, and Pring fears that the solutions pursued with such vigour by New Labour could be merely 'a continuation of a long line of "reforms" which do not work' (p. 50). He draws attention to the legacy of previously failed 14–19 initiatives and criticises New Labour for making an 'even more confusing array of qualifications, at different levels, than it had inherited' (p. 46). He also points to the often contradictory aspects of New Labour's education policies, such as encouraging greater school autonomy while requiring more partnerships. He believes that, in this phase as in others, the 'language of management' has increased alongside 'policy busyness' and suggests that 'this changed language of education may be one of the major legacies of the Blair years' (p. 49). Pring concludes that a holistic approach to the 14–19 phase is commendable but feels that at best the legacy might merely be a greater understanding of the issues, rather than the specific solutions offered by the Blair government.

John Furlong regards making teaching a 21st-century profession as Tony Blair's big prize (pp. 88–100). His paper focuses on changes to the teaching profession under New Labour and identifies both positive and negative aspects of Blair's policy. He notes that 'at the end of his term of office, there were more teachers, and they were more diverse in terms of their backgrounds than before; they were also better paid, better supported by teaching assistants and [perhaps] more highly regarded. But they were also much more managed than in the past' (pp. 97–98). He suggests that powerful mechanisms had been put in place to ensure that teachers, in their day-to-day practice, would 'conform to the centrally prescribed policy agendas and strategies, whether or not they agreed with them' (p. 98). Furlong asserts that it will take a long time for the real consequences of Blair's 'new professionalism' to be appreciated (p. 97), but suggests that Blair's real legacy in this field will be global with two widely cited international reports (the OECD report *Teachers Matter* (2005) and the McKinsey report (2007)) both being influenced by the last ten years of policies in England. However, he concludes by noting that Singapore is now adopting a more open form of teacher professionalism in its 'thinking schools', thus raising some doubts in his mind about whether the highly regulated New Labour approach is entirely appropriate for a 21st-century profession.

Neil Selwyn assesses the legacy of New Labour's ICT agenda and the extent to which it has realised the potential of new technology (pp. 63–74). In contrast to many of the other contributors, Selwyn does not find a great deal of continuity from Conservative policy in this area, claiming that 'New Labour can claim rightly to have made an unprecedented and sustained political commitment to technology in education since 1998' (p. 66). He takes the view that 'the New Labour ICT agenda was located firmly within wider prevailing concerns over enhancing competitiveness in a globalising economy and creating a lifelong learning system fit for a successful knowledge economy' (p. 70). Yet this was at the expense of pedagogical concerns and 'it was clear from the outset of the New Labour project that the economic rather than pedagogic significance of ICT was driving and shaping its implementation in the classroom' (p. 70). Even so, he regards the general aim of introducing ICT into education as having been successful and the UK's reputation in this respect as having been enhanced internationally. Nevertheless, Selwyn asserts that 'the much promised technology-based "transformation" of UK education has failed to materialise' (p. 67). He does not expect much to change in policy in the next ten years, regardless of the political party in government, claiming that 'it would seem that one of the strongest legacies of the 1997–2007 ICT agenda has been the opening up of ICT as an uncontested policy space' (p. 71).

David Gillborn discusses Tony Blair and the politics of 'race' in education (pp. 75–87) and argues that, despite some early progressive rhetoric, New Labour failed to address many significant issues. Indeed, after some apparent gains following the Stephen Lawrence Inquiry, there has subsequently been a regression to policies that are counterproductive and discriminatory. While some of the other papers also locate education policy within wider social and economic concerns, Gillborn almost totally subsumes it within Blair's broader approach to race. Like Walford in relation to faith schools, and Reay in relation to school choice, Gillborn considers Blair's personal role in policy, highlighting his commitments to both nationalism and meritocracy. He claims that 'despite its radical rhetoric, New Labour never moved beyond a superficial notion of equal opportunities; education policy simply could not accept that many fundamental assumptions that appear commonsensical (such as the nature of "ability") are actually deeply implicated in the creation and legitimation of racist educational inequality' (p. 84). Hence the government's use of 'colour-blind' targets and its 'love affair' with setting and 'giftedness' have never really been subjected to the sorts of impact assessment the government supposedly requires of all its policies.

While many of the papers focus on New Labour's record on schools, in 'Beyond tuition fees?' Ingrid Lunt considers the legacy of Blair's government for higher education (pp. 101–112). After describing in some detail policy towards higher education in the post-Dearing era, she suggests there is a tension between the market approach adopted by New Labour towards higher education and its avowed commitment to social justice, particularly in terms of widening participation. She argues that 'the New Labour agenda of enhanced global competiveness appears to have had a more significant impact on universities than its ideological commitment to social inclusion and equity while leaving fundamental challenges inherent in developing and financing a mass higher education system' (p. 110). She also identifies tensions between 'blue skies' research and 'applicable' research and between undergraduate and postgraduate teaching. Overall, Lunt believes that Blair's legacy is a highly marketised and stratified higher education system and that this has been more successfully implemented than the commitment to realising social justice in and through higher education.

Finally, David Reynolds focuses on an aspect of New Labour policy that is relatively neglected in the other contributions. In 'New Labour, education and

Wales: the devolution decade' (pp. 113–125), he demonstrates how the government's wider policy of devolution has impacted on education, especially in Wales which had until then remained close to the English model. In assessing the distinctively Welsh 'paradigm' of education policy that has emerged in recent years, he finds that this has a more community and less market and choice focused ethos than is currently fashionable both in England and internationally. Yet he shows that on many measures the English approach has been more successful. He suggests that an evaluation of the Welsh experience would tend to provide support for the English rather than the Welsh approach, arguing that 'it is difficult to avoid the conclusion that the legacy of devolution to Wales, and the policies that were followed after it, validate much of what can be called the New Labour educational paradigm of England. England spent more, prioritised more heavily and attended to the building of capacity more than Wales' (p. 123). However, he acknowledges that it remains unclear whether this was due to the failure of Welsh delivery mechanisms or to the policies themselves.

The tenor of the analyses

On hearing five of these papers at the 2008 BERA conference, I found myself in a strange position. Back in February 1998, early in Tony Blair's first administration, I had given a paper at Oxford University (at the invitation of Geoffrey Walford, as it happens) on 'New Labour, education and disadvantage'. This paper was subsequently published in a journal called *Education and Social Justice* (Whitty, 1998), edited by Richard Hatcher, another of the contributors to the 2008 symposium and the special issue. In that 1998 lecture, I had surprised the andience by saying that, unlike most people I knew in education, I had not danced on the streets in May 1997—either literally or metaphorically.

Walford, by contrast, confesses in his introduction to the special issue of the journal to having been 'particularly excited by Blair's now well-known three top priorities—education, education and education' (p. 1). Even at the time, I thought most people in education had had unrealistic expectations that New Labour would abandon most of the policies of Thatcher and Major. So I was not particularly surprised that Tony Blair led New Labour in England further down the path of privatisation than either of his two predecessors dared, nor that David Blunkett introduced degrees of prescription in the classroom that went far beyond the ambitions of Kenneth Baker in 1988 (see also Whitty, 2008). To that extent at least, I have some sympathy with the sub-text of papers such as those by Reay, Hatcher and Gillborn that it was probably naïve to expect too much change and that to do so was to misrecognise key aspects of the New Labour agenda.

Despite my relatively low expectations, I have in the intervening years been very critical of what I consider to be New Labour's most disappointing legacy, the failure significantly to narrow the gap between the educational outcomes for advantaged and disadvantaged pupils (Whitty, 2002; 2008). And, although Conservative Shadow Education Minister, Michael Gove, may have exaggerated the extent of that failure recently (Conservative Party, 2008; Gove, 2008), no one can regard the record as a good one, especially as it was so obvious to many of us that the neo-liberal policies being pursued in the first term of New Labour in education and elsewhere would have that effect. Indeed, when Ministers in more recent years have admitted that they have not made as much progress on that front as they might have done, I have reflected wryly on a pamphlet on the subject that Peter Mortimore and I wrote in 1997 (Mortimore & Whitty, 1997) and I have not always been able to resist the temptation to say 'We told you so'!

Yet a decade later, listening to the five papers presented at the BERA symposium, I felt very uneasy that the New Labour legacy was being presented in such negative terms. Indeed, my initial reaction to members of the disillusioned left educational establishment comprehensively deriding New Labour on virtually every front was that surely New Labour must have got something right! The predominantly negative impression of the papers may have arisen from the fact that speakers were dealing with discrete areas of policy about which they had particularly strong feelings. Only Reynolds seemed relatively positive about the Blair government's achievements in England but even that was in the context of a fairly damning critique of the effects of the alternative policies that had been pursued in Wales.

I am left with a similar impression of disillusionment with New Labour after reading all ten papers in the special issue, though they differ somewhat in the nature and extent of their critiques. Overall, half the papers take an overwhelmingly negative view of New Labour's achievements in their respective fields. The remaining papers provide a more mixed assessment and, importantly, these latter papers also display a greater appreciation of the dilemmas that the New Labour government has had to wrestle with and of the realities of the policy making process. Even so, the list of positive achievements identified by the authors is dwarfed by that of the more negative aspects. As we approach an election in which education policy will again be a major issue between the parties, I would have hoped that the contributors to the BERA symposium and the *Oxford Review of Education* would have provided a more nuanced evaluation of New Labour's record to date. In particular, I would have liked to see more recognition of those areas of policy in which there has been success and of those policies that are progressive in intent and at least potentially progressive in effect.

One difficulty is that it is not altogether clear in what terms the legacy is meant to be evaluated. Some of the contributors seem to assess it against their own hopes and expectations, while others assess it against the aims of New Labour or, more particularly, the ambitions of Tony Blair himself. While all the authors convey something of a sense of betrayal, these different approaches can lead to rather different assessments of the legacy. A few contributors offer us both. John Furlong, for example, concludes that Tony Blair 'was indeed successful in his ambitious attempts at reform' of the teaching profession, but questions whether the new model of professionalism that this entailed was 'the most appropriate one for the 21st century' (pp. 97–98). Hatcher, though, in what is one of the most critical contributions of all, both rejects the underlying assumptions of New Labour's policies and argues that they are failing even in their own terms.

Some common themes

So, while bearing in mind the differing orientations of the authors, how do they collectively sum up Blair's legacy in education? The one area about which most of those contributors who mention it—and some of them do not—are broadly positive is that of investment in education. They do acknowledge the huge increases in public expenditure on education over the past ten years. Two instances of this that stand out from the papers are the £5bn funding in the area of ICT infrastructure for schools (Selwyn) and increased support for teachers in terms of pay, training and the provision of teaching assistants (Furlong). The massive investment in Building Schools for the Future might also have been covered, while recognising that there have been some problems in the implementation of this imaginative programme (Education and Skills Committee, 2007). In England the overall increase in resources has been impressive. Expenditure on schools and early years provision increased by over 70% in real terms in ten years and that on higher education by nearly 30% (DCSF, 2008a). The figures for Scotland were also impressive—even before the current Scottish National Party government took power (Scottish Government, 2008). Increases in expenditure in Wales, as David Reynolds points out, have been more modest.

What comes through from the papers overall is that, despite major investments, a combination of misdirected expenditure and ideological confusion explains New Labour's failure to achieve its professed aim of high quality education for all. Sammons' paper illustrates this well but, unlike too many of the contributors, she recognises the enormity of the task New Labour faced and gives due credit for the successes that have been achieved. She is clear, for example, that there has been a great deal of school improvement under New Labour and that this means that a sustained reduction in the numbers of schools identified as weak or failing 'remains a substantive legacy' (p. 25). Thus, the number of schools where less than 30% of their pupils receive at least five GCSEs A*–C (including English and maths) fell from around 1,600 in 1997 to 638 in 2007. However, her praise is rightly tempered by a disappointment with the lack of success for the most disadvantaged pupils.

In fairness to New Labour, the importance of addressing the continuing failure of disadvantaged pupils was actually recognised by Estelle Morris as early as 2001 (DfES, 2001) and later given a particular emphasis by Ruth Kelly (Education and Skills Committee, 2006). Where I would agree with the majority of the contributors, though, is that New Labour has too often refused to accept that its own actions have sometimes hindered rather than helped in this respect. For example, some of the policies criticised by Reay have not always been sufficiently sensitive to structural and cultural limitations to parental choice. Similarly, as Sammons points out, even after introducing contextual value added measures, 'raw' test scores continued to be emphasised by Ministers, thereby understating the extraordinary success of some schools in increasing the achievement of disadvantaged pupils. Criticisms of this tendency certainly overshadowed the more positive aspects of the Brown government's National Challenge programme, which provides support for 'underachieving schools' in mainly disadvantaged areas, when it was first announced in 2008.

A recurring theme in the papers is thus the government's fixation on standards and target setting and the negative consequences of this. Sammons though sees some pluses in this approach even if she has reservations about some of the specific measures and the constant changes in what counts as 'success'. Gillborn criticises New Labour's preferred measures as naturally favouring particular (mainly white middle-class) pupils. Another common charge is that there has been an unhelpful increase in prescription by government in education. Pring argues that this reflects a belief that educational problems, which the government has 'identified', can be solved by central intervention and 'performance management' systems drawn from the world of commerce and business (p. 49), something that is arguably belied by the evidence even from that world.

Hatcher and others also note how the economic value of education, as opposed to its other benefits, is emphasised by New Labour. While many contributors recognise that there is a second key component of Blair's education policy rhetoric—social justice—they argue that this has too often been ignored at the expense of other priorities. Reay claims that middle-class power in the system has actually been strengthened, while Lunt questions the extent to which participation in higher education has really been widened.

A number of the authors suggest that New Labour has not done enough to address some pretty fundamental issues in education, leaving these matters to be picked up later or even by a different government. These include the role of faith schools (Walford), the need to resolve issues in the 14–19 phase (Pring) and the long-term funding of higher education (Lunt). This point is highlighted more generally by other authors in terms of New Labour's initial declaration to focus on 'standards not structures', thereby failing to address difficult matters such as the position of state grammar schools and the role of independent schools. The government itself might say that it has addressed these matters, but it has certainly not done so in a manner of which the contributors would approve.

An area in which there is a grudging recognition in the papers of New Labour's achievement is the international impact of New Labour's approach to education, which has been taken up or regarded favourably by overseas governments and international agencies. Such recognition feeds a New Labour obsession that its education system should be seen as 'world class'. Examples of 'success' in these terms are noted in the papers by Sammons, Furlong and Selwyn. However, given Britain's rather mixed performance in world performance tables and the concerns expressed by the contributors about the impact of these policies back home, this is more a tribute to New Labour's capacity to 'spin' than it is to its capacity to influence for the good.

The papers demonstrate very well that, as with the Thatcher administrations, much of the work of New Labour has been about trying to secure ideological change—for example, an ideological presence of ICT (Selwyn) and the creation of a pro-business habitus among Academy pupils (Hatcher) as part of a modernising agenda designed to enhance global competitiveness. Some of the papers also reveal conservative cultural assumptions in New Labour policies, albeit more muted ones than under previous Conservative governments. Their presence is clear, not only with regard to race, but also in the ways in which policies couched in rhetoric about global competitiveness and the realisation of talent actually play out in practice. There are hints of this in comments in the papers about gifted and talented programmes (Gillborn, Reay), 14–19 curriculum changes (Hatcher, Pring) and 'fair access' to élite universities (Lunt). Such assumptions are also part of the reason why the standards/excellence agenda so often seems to trump the social inclusion/equity agenda when the chips are down. This is perhaps why Every Child Matters has not so far had the impact it might have had.

There is, though, a tendency in the papers to question the motives of New Labour rather than to criticise the weakness of their understanding of the interaction between education and society. It is too easy to put New Labour's less than impressive legacy down to 'bad faith' or cynicism, though some of it may well be explicable in those terms. However, while not regarding the rhetoric of social justice as disingenuous, I do think New Labour can be criticised for a failure to grasp what it might take to make a significant inroad into disadvantage. It is also true that, had the government grasped this, it might not have been prepared to contemplate the far-reaching social consequences of implementing the necessary policies.

New Labour can perhaps be accused of hypocrisy in that, despite employing the rhetoric of evidence-based policy, it has too often preferred to appeal to commonsense rather than research evidence to justify the reforms—though we academics do tend to overstate the importance of our own craft in these matters (Whitty, 2006). But even appealing to commonsense rather than research evidence was not necessarily 'bad faith'. The commonsense that New Labour appealed to, such as that about ability that Gillborn talks about in his paper, was a commonsense that Blair, and at least some of his Secretaries of State, probably shared even as they played to it and perpetuated it. And, like all commonsense, it contained contradictory elements. This is also true of what Reay calls the 'middle-class psyche' epitomised by Blair.

Another problem for those who dissect policy and point out the confusions is that there is surely a sense in which the contradictory elements in its policies are what gave New Labour its widespread electoral appeal, certainly in England. If New Labour did do anything well, one of those things (at least until recently) was to produce policies that responded to the prejudices of swing voters in marginal constituencies without totally alienating Labour's traditional core voters.

Some of the difficulties in reconciling different aspects of New Labour policy almost certainly arose from Blair's own priorities, which were not always shared by his colleagues, and his extreme caution about what would play with the electorate. His own part in the rejection of the widely acclaimed Tomlinson proposals for the reform of 14–19 education was a case in point, while it is also highly questionable whether Blair himself would have sanctioned the abandonment of national testing at Key Stage 3, even after the marking debacle of 2008.

Beyond Blair

There are, therefore, those who hope that Gordon Brown's government will be better than Blair's at squaring the various circles confronting New Labour, not least because the new Prime Minister's personal agenda seems less at odds with Labour's social democratic past. There has already been some change in the mood music. The links between the school standards agenda and the children's agenda have been recognised in the formation of the Department for Children, Schools and Families (DCSF). Local authorities have acquired a role, albeit a limited one, in relation to the development of Academies, and regained some lost ground in further education funding. This suggests that there may eventually be more room again for local democracy in education. Other recent developments, such as the new Key Stage 3 curriculum and the abolition of national testing at age 14, could open up more space for professional judgement as the Blairite commitment to central prescription and market forces is seen to have run its course even in terms of raising standards.

Furthermore, Ministers have seemed genuinely outraged that a 'significant minority' of secondary schools failed to comply with the new Admissions Code (DCSF, 2008b). Indeed, they brought in new measures to monitor and police admissions practices, though these might not have been necessary if they had heeded Reay's research and had not made market competition between autonomous schools the key driver of the system. It is also positive that, although the government remains obsessed with targets, almost half of its current targets relate to closing the achievement gap between advantaged and disadvantaged groups (Baker, 2007).

However, as a leading political commentator put it when Blair stepped down, 'the Brown government will need courage and ingenuity to reconcile egalitarian ambitions with political realities' (Wilby, 2007). In so far as the contributors to the special issue have chosen to address this issue, they display little optimism that things are getting better under Brown. Selwyn, for example, argues that policy is still based on the economic case as opposed to egalitarian and social justice ones (p. 71). Whether the impact of the 'credit crunch' and Brown's consequent abandonment of some New Labour orthodoxies in relation to the banking system will produce similar revisionism elsewhere remains to be seen.

Conclusion

John Major once said that he shared Blair's priorities of 'education, education, education', but not necessarily in that order (Giddens, 2007, p. 62). This perhaps captures rather neatly the nature of Blair's legacy. It has certainly left us with a recognition at the highest levels of the crucial importance of education in contemporary society. However, while education moved to the centre of the policy stage, New Labour's priorities were too often misguided or at least confused and different parts of its policy agenda were in tension with each other.

Nevertheless, the Blair years left a positive legacy in terms of investment in education—and even in education research, as it happens. There was also real progress in early years provision, although there is still much to do on the quality of the early years workforce. Schools policy overall is more purposeful than before, but the foregrounding of the standards agenda at the expense of the inclusion agenda was a major problem in the first term in particular. However, Every Child Matters and the more recent Children's Plan did recognise that there is an important relationship between standards and the realities of children's lives outside school, though this has yet to be fully translated into coherent policies.

Meanwhile, is there anything the contributors might offer a future government in carrying forward this task? How might those potentially progressive policies that, according to their analyses, have been backgrounded under New Labour become foregrounded in the future? Unfortunately, there is surprisingly little about this in the papers in the special issue. This might be considered going beyond their brief, but the critiques offered in most of them are based on an implicit notion that things could have been done rather better.

One alternative to New Labour's English policies is, of course, the Welsh solution discussed by Reynolds. His list of Welsh policies reads like the wish list of the left educational establishment in England. The New Vision Group (http://www.newvisionsforeducation.org.uk/) has urged virtually all of those policies on the government at Westminster in the last few years. But, with a few caveats, the message from Reynolds is that they join a list of policies that have failed in Wales and, even if that is too harsh a judgement, the electorate in England is rather different from that in Wales and might not support such policies even if the evidence of their efficacy were more positive.

If a return to what Reynolds terms 'producerism' does not appear to be the answer, we desperately need some more imaginative thinking about alternatives from the academic left than we have here. Hatcher does offer us some Conservative scenarios after the election, but it would be a sad comment on the left-leaning academics who write in this collection if we now have to leave innovative thinking entirely to the Conservative Party or to its Civitas and Policy Exchange think tanks, even if the latter's recent advocacy of 'pupil premiums' (Freedman & Horner, 2008) is worth considering. Indeed, it is not so different from ideas put forward by Tim Brighouse to tackle disadvantage (Brighouse, 2009), although these were rejected by the government when he was Commissioner for London Schools. Hatcher, though, expects from the Conservatives essentially more of the same medicine as we have had from New Labour.

Hatcher is also the one contributor who offers us a glimpse of his own alternative scenario, which involves mass mobilisation against the neo-liberal agenda. However, before we can mobilise we surely need to be clearer what is to be mobilised around. Presumably not just past social democratic policies or even current ones in Wales, because neither of those options seem to provide a path to social justice, and neither of them would play particularly well with the contemporary commonsense of much of the English electorate.

So, finally, I would have liked to read more about what the alternatives to Blairite education policy might be and how a progressive commonsense might now be constructed and then mobilised around. In other words, can we now explore how we might build on what is positive, albeit backgrounded, in the New Labour legacy—and thereby move beyond critiques? Such an exercise could presumably draw on the findings of research carried out by the contributors themselves, as well as on the work of the DCSF's Effective Pre-School, Primary and Secondary Education Project (http://www.ioe.ac.uk/schools/ecpe/eppe/), the ESRC's Teaching and Learning Research Programme (http://www.tlrp.org/) and, in due course, the Institute of Effective Education at the University of York (http://www.york.ac.uk/iee/). Perhaps a future issue of the *Oxford Review of Education* could provide a forum for this.

Acknowledgements

I am grateful to David Reynolds and Geoffrey Walford for suggesting that I should develop my BERA conference response into a paper for this journal. I am also grateful to Amanda Sasia and Andrew Curtis for their help in preparing the response and to Emma Wisby for her helpful comments on an earlier draft.

References

Baker, M. (2007) Look where the target is pointing, BBC website, 20 October. Available online at: http://news.bbc.co.uk/1/hi/education/7052798.stm (accessed 3 January 2009).

Brighouse, T. (2009) All I want for education ..., *The Guardian* website, 2 January. Available online at: http://www.guardian.co.uk/education/2009/jan/02/tim-brighouse-wishlist (accessed 5 January 2009).

Conservative Party (2008) *A failed generation: educational inequality under Labour.* Policy paper. Available online at: www.conservatives.com/~/media/Files/Downloadable%20Files/A%20Failed%20Generation.ashx?dl=true (accessed 2 September 2008).

Department for Children, Schools and Families (DCSF) (2008a) *Departmental report 2008,* Cm 7391, May 2008 (London, The Stationery Office).

Department for Children, Schools and Families (DCSF) (2008b) Written ministerial statement on the Office of the Schools Adjudicator's Annual Report for 2007/08, Press Notice 2008/0243, 3 November.

Department for Education and Skills (DfES) (2001) *Schools: achieving success,* Cm 5230 (Nottingham, DfES Publications).

Education and Skills Committee (2006) *The schools white paper: higher standards, better schools for all,* Volume II—Oral and written evidence, HC 633-II (London, The Stationery Office).

Education and Skills Committee (2007) *Sustainable schools: are we building schools for the future? Seventh report of session 2006–07,* Volume I—Report, HC 140-I (London, The Stationery Office).

Freedman, S. & Horner, S. (2008) *School funding and social justice: a guide to the pupil premium* (London, Policy Exchange).

Giddens, A. (2007) *Over to you Mr Brown* (Cambridge, Polity Press).

Gove, M. (2008) Plight of forgotten pupils gets worse, *Times Educational Supplement* 8 August. Available online at: http://www.tes.co.uk/article.aspx?storycode=6000705 (accessed 2 December 2008).

McKinsey & Company (2007) *How the world's best performing school systems come out on top*. Available online at: http://www.mckinsey.com/clientservice/socialsector/resources/pdf/Worlds_School_Systems_Final.pdf (accessed 12 December 2008).

Mortimore, P. & Whitty, G. (1997) *Can school improvement overcome the effects of disadvantage?* (London, Institute of Education).

OECD (2005) *Teachers matter: attracting, developing and retaining effective teachers* (Paris, OECD).

Oxford Review of Education (2008) Special issue: 'Blair's Educational Legacy?' 34(6), 637–765.

Siraj-Blatchford, I., Taggart, B., Sylva, K., Sammons, P. & Melhuish, E. (2008) Towards the transformation of practice in early childhood education: the effective provision of pre-school education (EPPE) project, *Cambridge Journal of Education*, 38(1), 23–36.

Scottish Government (2008) *Statistics Publication Notice*. A National Statistics Publication for Scotland. Available online at: http://www.scotland.gov.uk/Resource/Doc/211797/0056333.pdf (accessed 2 January 2008).

Whitty, G. (1998) New Labour, education and disadvantage, *Education and Social Justice*, 1(1), 2–8.

Whitty, G. (2002) *Making sense of education policy: studies in the sociology and politics of education* (London, Sage).

Whitty, G. (2006) Education(al) research and education policy making: is conflict inevitable? *British Educational Research Journal*, 32(2), 159–176.

Whitty, G. (2008) Twenty years of progress? English education policy 1988 to the present, *Educational Management Administration and Leadership*, 36(2), 165–184.

Wilby, P. (2007) Why education remains the priority, *New Statesman*, 14 May, 14.

INDEX

Page numbers in **bold** and 'n.' or 'nn.' plus note number indicate figures/tables and notes respectively.

Enabling Reflective Learning in Lifelong Career Guidance

This book is based on a fieldwork intensive, EU funded project, aimed at sustaining the empowerment processes of career guidance practitioners by developing their awareness and use of their individual, organizational and networking resources. The field work activity was carried out in three different national contexts: Italy, Bulgaria and Switzerland, and based on a creative methodological approach called Participative and Appreciative Action and Reflection (PAAR).

The contributions cover a wide range of intertwined subjects. These include: (a) deep reflection on life long career guidance (LLCG) systems and processes in the three national contexts involved; (b) the challenges of managing PAAR projects in organisations; (c) the role of a participative and appreciative approaches in facilitating a positive shift from professionals inside welfare state institutions, to a more counselling oriented mission; (d) how to build up an appreciative memory that is a way of representing experience and creating space for relationships so that they remain stable over time; (e) reflection on what may happen to learning processes if the contexts in which the empowerment practices are implemented happen through a virtual environment such as a blog or a social network. The editors are all experienced researchers and practitioners working if the field of facilitation, life long career guidance, counselling, reflective learning and social innovation.

This book was originally published as a special issue of *Reflective Practice: International and Multidisciplinary Perspectives.*

Ruggiera Sarcina is a Senior Consultant, Facilitator and Researcher and Vice President of Reflective Learning Italy. Her main fields of expertise concern project management, action learning and facilitation techniques especially in the framework of European projects, small- and medium-sized enterprises (in particular, aggregation path for innovation and internationalisation projects) and local development.

Simona Marchi is the General Director of SMILE Italy (System, Methodology, Innovation, in Education) and President of Reflective Learning Italy, 2008-2012. She was a Temporary Researcher at Sapienza, University of Rome, Italy from 2001 to 2009 and has authored papers on research methods, reflective learning, participative change and innovation in organizations, learning by using web resources.

Furio Bednarz is President and Responsible for R&D by ECAP Foundation Switzerland and President of the Conference of CVT Organisation of Italian speaking Switzerland. His research focuses on labour market and workplace evolution, migrations, competence development and innovative training and experiential learning methods.

Massimo Tomassini is a Social Scientist and Mindfulness Trainer. Massimo is Contract Professor at the University of Roma 3, Italy (teaching organisational learning) and

Associate Fellow at the Institute for Employment Research, University Warwick, UK. With the latter he is at present partner in a transnational research aimed at interpreting individual work and learning paths in different contexts. As a private consultant, he carries out both counseling activities and mindfulness training workshops for individuals and groups.

Galina Markova, PhD. is Director of Know How Centre for Alternative Care for Children at the New Bulgarian University. She graduated from the doctoral program of Smith College School for Social Work, USA and her research is in the field of child welfare and de-institutionalization of services for children, program evaluation in post-totalitarian context, international social work. She is also an educator and clinician in private practice.

Francesco Consoli has been Associate Professor of Sociology of Organization, Sociology of Professions and Sociology of Innovation at La Sapienza, University of Rome, Italy. He has a long experience in reflexive practices and methodologies in teaching and training. In this field he published several articles and books on education and reflective practices. He participated in two Leonardo da Vinci Projects: 'Reflect' (2004-2006) and 'Reflect-OR' (2009-2010).